NAKLADATELSTVÍ

CORPORATION

FOREIGNERS IN PRAGUE

JOSEF HRUBEŠ
EVA HRUBEŠOVÁ

NAKLADATELSTVÍ

ORION
CORPORATION

$\mathcal{D}$EAR READERS,

Encouraged by our readers' response to the three volumes of our publication, *The Houses of Prague Tell Stories*, we have gone over the many sources in our extensive library and archives once more to compile this narrative publication on a particularly interesting Pragensist theme – famous foreigners in Prague. Over the many centuries of Prague's history, this city of 100 spires has been visited by hundreds of prominent personages. Some of them came to stay for just a little while, others stayed longer or made Prague their second home. This book presents selected visitors to Prague in the form of brief accounts of their personal lives and stories associated with their individual visits to Prague. No particular rules or criteria were applied in choosing the personalities for this book – we only have tried to present a colorful gallery of personages from all walks of life.

The authors

Hans Christian

$\mathcal{A}$NDERSEN

L et us begin in style to do justice to the memory of Hans
Christian Andersen (1805 - 1875), the uncrowned king
of a quite specific literary genre - fairy tales. Well, in
1805, in a little tiny room, there lived a newlywed couple,
a shoemaker and his wife, who loved one another very much.
The husband was barely twenty-two, extremely gifted, a real
poet at heart. His wife, who was his senior by a few years, had
no knowledge of the ways of the world, but she had a sincere
heart. Of course, we have borrowed both of the above
sentences from Andersen's autobiography which wrote in his
latter days. We know for a fact that we was born on April 2,
1805 in a small Danish village called Odense.

It is said that his birth took place in a bed made by his father
out of a catafalque which had at one time stood under the coffin
of some wealthy man. A fortune-teller reportedly told his
mother: "Your son shall be like a wild bird. He shall fly very high
and achieve admiration worldwide. And on one beautiful day,
Odense shall welcome him with festive lights." The fulfillment

of that prophesy was then a long way off, for Andersen was to live a very busy life before it would come true.

In 1819, he left the place of his birth for Copenhagen, three years after the death of his father who, in an attempt to help the financial situation of the family, had enlisted in the Napoleon's army only to return in a state of failing health. In Copenhagen Andersen first tried his luck as an actor in a theater, but was eventually forced to admit that he had absolutely no talent for acting.

At that point he decided to try his luck in the art of writing. Having started out as a poet, he eventually became a playwright, and even a novelist. His best known works of that period were *The Improviser, To Be or Not To Be, O.Z.*, and a book of short stories titled *The Pictureless Picture Book*. He met his luck in the person of Jonas Collin, the director of the Royal Theater, who, perhaps having anticipated his great literary talent, took him under his wing and enabled him to study.

But the heart of the 25-year-old poet began to open itself to love. It must be said that the love of his life was as intense as it was unhappy. Andersen fell in love with the brown-eyed Riborg Voigt, his junior by one year, despite knowing that she was already engaged to a young ranger. Due to this, he was quickly refused and, soon thereafter, his loved one confirmed the engagement by marrying. Besides, it is said that Andersen was extraordinarily homely and looking at his portrait of 1905, published in the *Zlatá Praha* (Golden Prague) magazine, we see no reason to question it.

His disappointment was so great he was devastated. But he happened to have a friend who showed him how to forget. The remedy was supposed be a journey abroad, according to the unwritten rule: out of sight, out of mind. Andersen listened to his advice and traveling amused him so much that he not only spent several months abroad every year since, but also found it inspiring enough to write about it.

During his travels throughout Europe, he visited Bohemia several times, including Prague on 3 occasions. He particularly liked Northern Bohemia, so-called Bohemian-Saxon Switzerland. He was excited over the nature in that region, he admired the Pravčická brána (Pravčice Arc) and Hřensko. His unique impressions from the area are described in his book titled *Shadow Pictures of Travels from Hartz to Bohemian-*

Saxon Switzerland, etc., written in the summer of 1831. Although he had, thanks to his extensive trips, eventually become an experienced globetrotter, qualified to make valid comparisons, nothing could override his affection for this part of the world where he always liked to return.

It was August 1834 when Andersen came to Prague for the first time. Originally planning just an informative two-day trip, he was so taken by the city that he extended his trip to five days. He viewed the Prague Castle and explored the then still unfinished St. Vitus Cathedral.

It was here, as he bragged in his letter from Prague, dated August 18, 1834, that he happened to meet the Duke of Angoulme, a member of the French royalty in exile, who was living in Prague with his wife, having been granted a temporary asylum in Prague by the Austrian Imperial Court. In the same letter, he admits that he liked the ladies and young women in Prague. He confesses that when sitting in a covered carriage, in deep anonymity, he occasionally could not hold back and would yell out in passing: "Beautiful girl, I love you!"

Out of the palaces in Prague, he was most thrilled by the Valdštejnský palác (Wallenstein Palace) and its vast gardens. He was particularly strongly impressed by the Jewish Ghetto which he visited as well. The narrow, overcrowded, crooked streets, interesting personalities, and life itself which, as it appeared to a random visitor, was happening right in the street. His impressions were intensified by a visit to the Old-New Synagogue and the Old Jewish Cemetery.

Hans Christian Andersen visited Prague the second time in 1841. He visited the various points of interest, again, including the St. Vitus Cathedral, where he took a particular interest in the ornate silver tombstone of St. Jan Nepomuk and the story of his fate. In Old Town Prague he was very touched at the sight of another prominent tombstone over the grave of one of his countrymen, Tycho Brahe, at Virgin Mary's Church.

Contemplating the fact that this great man, an astronomer at the Court of Emperor Rudolf II, repudiated by his own country, had to be laid at rest in a grave so far from home, Andersen wept in the silent aisle of the Cathedral. He mentions this visit of Prague in his book of travels titled *The Poet's Bazaar*.

It is certainly an interesting detail that, on his way home, he took a boat from Prague to Dresden, a wooden paddle steamer called *Bohemia*. The boat had been built in Prague by British engineers, A. Andrews and J. Ruston. Measuring 37 meters in length, the boat was propelled by a two-cylinder steam engine with a performance of 23 kW. This flat–bottomed vessel could carry up to 140 persons. When fully loaded, including fuel, *Bohemia* had an extremely high load-line - only one half meter. At that time, passengers would be taken to Obříství by stagecoach and continue to Dresden by boat, but Andersen took the boat directly from Prague. He was very happy to have made that choice as it allowed him not only to enjoy the beauty of the Bohemian countryside, but also enabled him to admire technical evolution in progress firsthand. It should be added that *Bohemia* traveled under Austrian colors and its stern was covered with a canvas roof to protect the passengers from foul weather and soot which was being emitted in large quantities from the enormous smokestack.

During the periods between journeys, Andersen worked on his writings - little did he anticipate that they would bring him immortality. In addition to novels, poems, and travel books, he wrote fairy tales - his favorite genre. During his fruitful life, he wrote 150 of them. Most of them have become children's favorites, generation after generation, and they are being read by adults all over the world as well. Let us recall - to name a few - *The Ugly Duckling, The Nightingale, The Fir-Tree, Flint and Steel, The Snow Queen, The Princess and the Pea, Wild Swans. The Little Mermaid*, and lesser known fairy tales like *The Little Thumb Boy, Little Claus and Big Claus*, and we could go on...

The third and final time that Hans Christian Andersen visited Prague was in March 1866. This time he took a stagecoach from Dresden. His host in Prague was Count Thun. The year 1866 was a year of war for the Austro-Hungarian Empire, so Andersen took a train when returning from Prague. The train was full of soldiers who were being transferred to Poland, where civil unrest had broken out. In his letter about this trip, he wrote, among other things: "We went on and on through tunnels, across viaducts, the windows rattling, the whistle signals sounding, the engine heavily puffing... I leaned my head against the wall of my compartment and fell asleep entrusting myself to the guardianship of God."

The words of the fortune-teller about Andersen's destiny

were to be fulfilled to the last detail. Beyond that, however, it remains to be stated that even though his fairy tales feature princesses galore, he had never met his princess in all his life. The world-famous fairy-tale author, Hans Christian Andersen, died on June 31, 1875. His funeral, held in the Fraue Kirke Church in Copenhagen, was attended even by the Danish King and Queen, members of the Parliament, many other prominent personages an dignitaries, and, above all, a countless number of sincere admirers of his literary works.

Just like Prague is proud of Andersen's visits, so is Copenhagen even more proud of having been Andersen's home town. There are many places where a visitor to Copenhagen may encounter his images - at the Wax Museum in the Tivoli Amusement Park, but mainly on Andersen Avenue, where his statue stands. The famous Dane sits there, dressed in period clothing, wearing a bowler hat and, holding a book in his hand, he is telling one of his fairy tales. Maybe it is the one about the Little Mermaid, whose statue, created by Edward Eriksen in 1913, sitting on a rock at the seashore, has become an inseparable symbol of the capital city of Denmark.

Fr. Hoogenberghe: Panorama of Hradčany, view from Letná;
engraving from Vol. V of *CIVITATES ORBIS TERRARUM* by
Georgius Braun, Cologne on the Rhine, about 1595, detail
(Prague - National Museum)

Joachim

BARRANDE

O ver the long period of its existence, the National Museum, an institution so dear to all Czechs, had not only countless supporters, but also many sponsors, as well as major and minor donors. One of the most notable among them was a French construction engineer, geologist, and paleontologist, Joachim Barrande, the founder of Czech paleontology.

The future world-famous scientist was born on August 11, 1799, in a little French town called Saugues in southern France. As a young man, he graduated from the Faculty of Civil Engineering at the Polytechnical Institute in Paris. He was equally interested in natural sciences, which he studied simultaneously, perhaps not even realizing that they were to become his lifelong destiny and mission. Thanks to his scholarly accomplishments, Joachim Barrande was offered a great honor and opportunity when he was invited to the Royal Court to become a teacher and educator of Henry de Chambord, a grandson of the French King Charles X. This assignment, however, was to be only a temporary one.

The July Revolution in 1830 deprived Charles X of his throne and he, along with his family, was forced to leave France. At first, they settled in Edinburgh, Scotland, but soon thereafter they gratefully accepted an invitation from the Austrian Emperor, Franz I, to move to Bohemia. The story of the French royal family is of interest to us primarily because the family brought also Joachim Barrande to Bohemia, to the Prague Castle, where the exiled ex-monarch was given shelter. During the time spent in Prague, Barrande gradually became acquainted with the leading scientists of the time, e.g., František Palacký, who tutored the young French prince in German; Joseph Dobrovský; two mineralogists, František Xaver Zip and Antonín Frič; but also Count Kaspar of Sternberg, who not only was devoted to natural sciences, but also generously sponsored them.

In 1833, Joachim Barrande was released from his teaching duties, reportedly on the grounds of his opinions which were, according to his employers, too liberal and therefore unsuitable for the young Prince. Barrande had to move out of the Prague Castle to house no. 36, called *U Flavínů* [Flavin's House], sometimes also *U Splavínů*, situated at Malostranské náměstí [Malá Strana Square] No. 36, which features a large mural depicting Virgin Mary's Coronation on its facade. Suddenly jobless, Barrande was saved by one of his acquaintances, Count Kaspar of Šternberk [Sternberg], who offered him a position as a civil engineer on the construction of an extension of the Prague-Lány horse-driven railway to Radnice, a new coal-mining basin to be opened. The offer was gratefully accepted, for it provided Barrande with adequate existential provisions.

We shouldn't forget to mention that, during his educational activities, Barrande would take long walks to the outskirts of Prague, in areas of untouched nature. At that time, if one walked towards the South, just past the Újezd gate, there were orchards, meadows, and vineyards everywhere. During one such outing, having crossed a village called Zlíchov, he came to a very romantic valley called Prokopské údolí. It was here, in a gorge, that he made a most interesting find - two fossils of *Pygidium Trilobite Odontochile Rugosa*. This random find, which may have partly been a stroke of destiny, changed completely Barrande's life, determining the direction that his scientific explorations would take.

During the surveys and digs, performed as part of setting the route for the above mentioned railway extension (which was, according to plan, to continue all the way to Pilsen, but never realized, a large quantity of fossils were found, predominantly around Skryjí and Týřov, mostly trilobites and other hitherto unknown faunal species. Barrande began to systematically collect these finds, describing them and analyzing them scientifically. For these purposes, he engaged a permanent circle of assistants, construction workers, and masons from local quarries. They would bring him their finds and Barrande would pay small amounts of money for them. He even tried to form a network of his own workers, paid by the hour, but was forced to abandon this system as it proved to be uneconomical. As his collection kept growing, his apartment in Prague began to be cluttered with boxes of fossiles.

Eventually, he changed employment, too, becoming a manager of Chambord properties, owned by Henry de Chambord, Joachim Barrande's former student during his teaching career. Also, this new employment provided him with enough time and subsistence to enable him to search in the territory of Central Bohemia for evidence of fossilized inhabitants of an ancient sea in the area. By then, Barrande had also moved to a five-room apartment in house no. 419 on the corner of today's Vítězná třída [Victory Avenue]. Today, the house bears a commemorative plaque which was ceremoniously unveiled in 1969 in his memory. The plaque also features the scientist's bust and an imprint of a trilobite. An interesting detail is that Barrande's housekeeper happened to have been the mother of Jan Neruda, who also taught him Czech. Barrande liked her very much and called her Babette, a diminutive of her actual name, Barbora. In her honor, he named one of the trilobites *Babinka Prima*. He met Barbora Neruda at the Prague Castle, where she had been a servant to Duke Guiche, who was sharing his exile in Prague with the French Royal Court.

Joachim Barrande not only diligently collected fossils, he also analyzed them scientifically. In 1852, he began to publish his life's work, *The Silurian System*, of Central Bohemia. 22 volumes of 6000 pages each, complemented by 1160 lithographic plates with illustrations were published during his life. The plates were created by his friend, Ladislav Pinkas, a Prague attorney, who was living in Sovovy Mlýny [Sova's Mills] on the Kampa nearby, and who is also known as the father of the painter Soběslav Pinkas.

To express his affection for the Czech people and their language, he frequently used Czech names, in addition to scientifically mandatory Latin terminology. That's why names like *Vlasta, Královna, Kropenatý ocásek, Pantata, Synek*, or *Tenka* have been preserved to this day. One of his exemplars even got the name of one Bedřich Smetana's operas, *Prodaná nevěsta*, i.e., *Panenka Vendita* [Bartered Bride].

Joachim Barrande achieved well-deserved recognition already during his life. Highly respected as a merited scholar, he was invited to participate in scientific activities in the country as well as abroad. Every year, he would go to Paris to attend the annual conference of the French Geological Society. Apart from these events, he maintained a very modest lifestyle, so completely taken up by his scientific research that he never even found time enough to marry. Since his apartment was packed with his collections, he would spend most of his time in his kitchen which doubled as a living room and a study.

In the Fall of 1883, already an old man of 84, Joachim Barrande went to Frohsdorf, Austria, south of Vienna. He wanted to visit his one-time student, Count Henry de Chambord, who was gravely ill. The biting-cold, damp weather, typical for that season of the year was fatal to him. Already during the trip to Austria he fell ill with pneumonia and so it happened that he survived the patient, whose suffering he had wanted to ease, by only a few days. Joachim Barrande died on October 5, 1883. He was buried in the cemetery of a nearby town, Lanzenkirchen, about 50 km from Vienna. At the present, his grave is in a fairly poor condition. The tall tombstone is badly damaged so that the inscription containing his biographical data and describing his scientific accomplishments is no longer legible.

Let us now return to what was hinted at in the beginning: Joachim Barrande left a testament, in which he designated the National Museum in Prague, the Czech nation's most prominent representative of science, to be his universal beneficiary. In his testament he stated simply: "The fossils in my collection come from the Bohemian soil, hence they belong to the Bohemian country." The significance of this endowment can hardly be appreciated enough, for the collection counts almost 300,000 petrified specimen in 1,200 crates, containing 50,000 types of original specimen. An integral part of this generous bequest was also Barrande's unique scientific library, his diaries, and notes. All that was topped with a monetary gift in the amount of 10,000 guilders, which were to be used for the completion of Barrande's life-work, *The Silurian System of Central Bohemia*. Barrande's bust, with the ever-present trilobite engraved in the plinth, situated in a place of honor at the National Museum, symbolizes a tribute to his personality and scientific activities. His collection is on display in the National Museum.

Already a year after Barrande's death, his friends and supporters had a large plate, well visible from a great distance, placed very high up on one of the rocks between Zlíchov and Malá Chuchle. They justified their choice as follows: "... it may have been right here that Barrande found his first fossil." The geological formation spreading westwards of Prague, roughly in the direction of Pilsen, was named Barrandien, in his memory. Likewise, the suburban section of Prague, where an affluent residential settlement, large film studios, and several terrace restaurants were built during the period between WW I and WW II, bears a name in his memory - Barrandov.

In 1983, i.e., 100 years after Barrande's death, this anniversary was put in the cultural calendar of UNESCO.

Fr. Hoogenberghe: Panorama of Malá Strana, view from Letná;
engraving from Vol. V of *CIVITATES ORBIS TERRARUM* by
Georgius Braun, Cologne on the Rhine, about 1595, detail
(Prague - Namunicipal Museum)

Ludwig van

BEETHOVEN

I f one wants to take a walk from Maltézské náměstí [Maltese
Square] on Malá Strana to Mostecká Street, one has to
pass through Lázeňská Street. Unless deep in thought,
one is bound to notice a conspicuous commemorative plaque on
the front of house no. 285/II, named *U Zlatého jednorožce*
[Golden Unicorn]. Imprinted in the relief of the plaque is the
likeness of an ingenious music composer, Ludwig van
Beethoven (1770 - 1827) and the inscription next to it says:
"Here, at the Golden Unicorn, the famous music composer,
Ludwig van Beethoven was a guest in 1796." The plaque is the
work of a Prague sculptor, carver, and medallist, Otakar Španiel.
It was put in its place in 1927 as part of the events which took
place on the occasion of the 100th anniversary of the
composer's death.

The number of Beethoven's visits to Prague is relatively
small, not counting his occasional passing through Prague on
his way to a spa in North Bohemia. Quite uncertain is a report
of his stay in Prague in 1795, where he is said to have held

a Christmas piano concert at the invitation of the Bohemian gentry. The sole mention of this event, even though a very brief one, is found in Dlabač's *Artists Lexicon*, plus a few scanty hints in Beethoven's personal correspondence. We can therefore presume, for presumption it is in the first place, that the artist was staying in Prague in February 1796 and then again in 1798, during which time he actively participated in the Autumn season of concerts in Prague.

Ludwig van Beethoven was christened on December 17, 1770, in Bonn. The date of his christening substitutes the date of his birth, as was common in those days, meaning that he was born just a few days before that date. At that time, unfortunately, a very high percentage of children died shortly after birth, so all parents hurried to have their babies christened as soon as possible, so that their tiny tot would not, in the worst scenario, die without being christened. Generally, according to confirmed cases, christening would take place about three days after birth and that would be the date entered in the Register of Births.

Beethoven was, due to his obvious, extraordinary talent, considered a child prodigy. He already performed publicly at an early age of eight years. In 1792, he moved with his parents from his native Bonn to Vienna, where he settled for good. He became a brilliant musician, pianist, music teacher, and composer and he was soon recognized as such in all the music salons of Vienna. Through music he became acquainted with the cream of the society of the time, i.e., the rich burghers and the aristocracy. And since music unites nations, and did so even in those days, among his friends were also Bohemian musicians.

In the society of those days, a music composer and concert master had to tend to his relations with the aristocracy, above all. The aristocracy had a great deal of interest, and a very sincere one, it must be added, in the concerts of prominent musicians, constantly demanding new music pieces and organizing musical events. Prague was no exception to this custom. In February 1796, Beethoven was invited to the City of 100 Spires on the Vltava River by Christian Philip, Count of Clam-Gallas. The private concerts of the Clam-Gallas' were held in a noble piano salon over the entrance to their magnificent aristocratic residence, Palace No. 158 on Husova Street in Old Town Prague. Beethoven also gave concerts in the guest palace of the aristocratic family Clary-Aldringen, in House No. 16 at Valdštejnské náměstí [Wallenstein Square] on Malá Strana. At one of the small banquets which used to follow the concerts, the composer made many a useful contact. One of them, with an enthusiastic, non-professional musician and composer, JUDr. Jan Nepomuk Kaňka, otherwise a well-reputed judicial court official, turned out to be particularly useful at a later time.

A Prague painter and portraitist, landscape and still-life painter, Martin Tejček (1781 - 1849), depicted Beethoven as a content-looking burgher-like gentleman, standing upright, dressed in a black loosely-fitting garb, a white vest with a shirt-front, and a massive silk-top hat on his curly head. In his hands, held behind his back, he clasped a clear attribute of his trade - a rolled-up music sheet. In 1940, the portrait was in the possession of a well-known Pragensist and writer, Dr. Karel Hádek. He published it in his book titled *Readings of Old Prague*.

During his stay in Prague, Beethoven was a joyful young man, with a tendency to joke. We can verify that in a part of a letter written by him from Prague to his Czech friend, a brilliant violoncellist, music conductor, composer, and co-founder of the Viennese Society of Music Friends, Vincenc Houšek. Among other things, he wrote: "Enjoy, dear bum, may you have a smooth movement on your beautiful potty." To Countess Karolina Kinsky, who asked him, whether he often visited Mozart's operas, he retorted with irony in his voice: "No, Madam. I fear for my originality."

But Ludwig van Beethoven encountered in Prague something quite serious - love. One day, he was invited to the Malá Strana palace of Count Clary, who asked him to teach his 19-year-old daughter on the piano. At first, Beethoven refused, saying he was too busy with his concert schedule. But when the Count introduced his daughter to him, everything was suddenly different - Beethoven agreed. During the lessons, he fell hopelessly in love with his student, despite knowing that the Countess was already engaged to Count Christian Christopher of Clam-Gallas, son of his Prague host. He even composed a two-page music piece for her, titled *"Pour la belle J. par L.v.B."* ("For beautiful Josephine from Ludwig van Beethoven."). The moment of truth came when he handed the music piece to her. The stunned beauty abruptly refused to accept it, saying that she honored Beethoven strictly as an excellent musician, and left the room. The humiliated composer left Prague, deeply hurt at heart. The next time he visited Prague, Josephine was already married to her then fiancé.

The next Beethoven's stay in Prague, probably his second, dates back to the fall of 1798. By then, he was also giving concerts to the music-loving public. One of his concerts given at the Konvikt Hall, the then sanctuary of music at Bartolomějská Street in Old Town Prague, was particularly memorable. He began his performance in the packed academy by playing his piano *Concert in C-major, No.15*, then continued with *Adagio* and graceful *Rondo* from his *Concert in A-major, No. 2*. To conclude his brilliant performance he played an improvised fantasy on the theme of Mozart's *La Clemenza di Tito: "Ah tu fosti il primo oggetto."* The concert was attended by a prominent Czech music composer of the pre-Smetana era, Václav Jan Tomášek (1774 - 1850). He wrote about it later in his autobiography, "Beethoven's magnificent performance, especially his daring rendition of fantasy shook me extraordinarily. My, I felt humiliation so profound that I could not as much as touch my piano for several days. Only irresistible love for music - and my rationality - could encourage me to practice even more diligently." The enormous success of Beethoven's performance had a strong impact on others, as well, and the Master had to give one more concert at everybody's request.

Beethoven's permanent residence was in Vienna, but he used to pass through Prague frequently on his way to the spas in North Bohemia and West Bohemia, where he was treated for his unstable mental condition and gradually advancing deafness. To make life even harder, he began to have material problems. In honor of his genius, his noble patrons, Ferdinand Jan Kinsky and Joseph Franz Lobkowitz, had bestowed him with an annuity of 4,000 guilders, each, to which Archduke Rudolf of Hapsburg added a little more. On account of this pension, Beethoven refused a well-paid position of a conductor in Kassel. But everything changed - in 1811, the Austrian currency crashed, Kinsky died a year later, Lobkowitz lost much of his wealth and the annuity payments from his estate were suspended. At that time, Beethoven turned for help to his Pragonian admirer, attorney Jan Nepomuk Kaňka. Since this lawyer happened to be the executor of Kinsky's estate and also handled the legal affairs of the Lobkowitz family, he managed to exact the promised funds on Beethoven's behalf, after three long years of court proceedings, so that the payment of the annuity was eventually resumed.

Prague's history lovers are well familiar with the Malá Strana house No. 210, named *U tří housliček* [House of 3 Fiddles], in the lower section of the steep Neruda Street. The front facade of the house features three violins in memoriam of three prominent violin-making families that used to exercise their craft in that house. It is probably not too far-fetched to assume that one of those masters was Jan Jiří Helmer, whose superbly built instruments were reportedly on par with Italian ones. Even Beethoven acquired one of his masterpieces.

Ludwig van Beethoven, a music genius, composer, and piano virtuoso, author of many immortal compositions, such as the *Ninth Symphony, Fateful Symphony,* piano concerts, and other compositions, went completely deaf towards the end of his life, and died on March 26, 1827, in Vienna. But his music is immortal.

Let us recall one more story linked to Beethoven's work - a very recent story with a happy end. On September 1996, an article in *Pražské noviny* [Prague News] printed the following message: "Beethoven's manuscript retrieved. The original of Beethoven's score of the *Moonlight Sonata* for the piano, stolen from the Benešov State Regional Archives in 1994 and smuggled to Germany, was returned yesterday to the archives administration of the Ministry of the Interior in Prague by Jiří Gruša, the Czech Republic's Ambassador to Germany. Beethoven's autograph had been offered for sale to J. A. Stargardt, an auction company in Berlin. Thanks to said auction company's decent attitude and cooperation with Berlin criminologists, mediated by the Czech Embassy, the rare archival document was returned to the Czech Republic. According to information from the Ministry of the Interior, the manuscript will be re-deposited in the family files of the Chotka Fund at the State Regional Archives in Prague."

Roelant Savery: Čertovka under the Stone Bridge (Charles
Bridge); watercolor- pen-ink drawing, about 1610, detail (Prague
- Municipal Museum)

Joseph

BERGLER

T he painter Joseph Bergler Jr., a native of Salzburg (1753 -
1829), was the first director in the history of the Fine
Arts Academy in Prague. He was born on May 1, 1753,
in the family of a well-known sculptor Joseph Bergler (1718 -
1788). At the time of his son's birth, Joseph Bergler Sr. was
providing services to the local gentry and diocese in Passau, in
addition to his Salzburg activities. His specialization was
decorative sculpture. Upon being appointed as court sculptor in
that tiny ecclesiastic state, he moved his family to Passau.
Joseph Bergler Jr. was brought up in that environment from
a very early age. The Rudolfinum Gallery of Friends of Fine Arts
at one time owned two busts of a Passau Bishop, Leopold
Arnost Firmian, made by Joseph Bergler Sr..

An enthusiastic fan of Joseph's father, this clerical dignitary
was the person most responsible for young Joseph
Bergler's being sent from Passau to Italy, where he studied and
worked from 1776 until 1786. Well endowed with artistic skills
by his father, young Joseph took lessons in drawing, painting,

and mural painting with M. Knoller and A. Maron. He also studied antique models and copied famous Italian masters' works to learn their craft. Upon finishing his studies, he returned to Passau to become the court painter of Bishop Leopold Leonard, Count von Thun-Hohenstein (1748 - 1826), member of a prominent aristocratic family whose roots reached also to Bohemia. Two years after his resettlement to Passau, Joseph Bergler Jr. was to carry out a very sad duty: namely, to bury his father, Joseph Bergler Sr., his first teacher and mentor in fine arts.

During the time when Joseph Bergler Jr. continued his services for the Bishops of Passau, an institution called Society of Patriotic Friends of Fine Arts was founded on Feb. 8, 1796, in Prague. First, the Society opened a gallery which was to become the National Gallery later, and soon thereafter the Society focused on educational activities, concentrating on the preparation of future artists. With this goal in mind, on Sept 10, 1799, the following year, the Society opened a school of fine arts in the premises of a one-time Jesuit building, called Klementinum, where it stayed until 1886.

Having organized all the fundamentals involved in the establishment of the school, the Society had to find a solution for the most essential problem: a suitable director and leading personality in fine arts, all in one person. Their attention turned towards Passau, to a German painter, drawer, and engraver, Joseph Bergler. However, to win the Master's agreement would not suffice in those days. The Society of Patriotic Friends of Fine Arts had to ask Bishop Leopold Leonard, Count von Thun-Hohenstein to release Bergler from service, so that a contract could be signed with him for a period of 4 - 6 years in the new location. The Bishop agreed and a contract between the parties, the Society and Joseph Bergler, was signed on April 8, 1800. The Society undertook, among other contractual obligations, to pay Bergler 700 guilders upon his arrival in Prague, in quarterly intervals. Furthermore, he was to get a five-room apartment in the Klementinum, free of charge, and the Society was to ensure all the conditions necessary for the smooth operation of the fine arts school. Bergler, on his part, undertook to provide the School with study sketches and drawings, especially such as he had drawn himself during his stay in Italy, and to teach his students to draw and paint from live models and real nature.

Though a foreigner, Bergler fully assimilated with the Bohemian cultural environment. In his water-color series of the period between 1801 and 1802, he even developed interest in Bohemian history. His paintings, e.g., *Libuše's Tribunal, Oldřich and Božena,* or *The Rescue of Charles IV in Pisa,* show a certain degree of Romanticism, despite their Classicist academic appearance. Although his primary mission in Prague was to teach, as will be elaborated on later, Bergler left a relatively rich legacy in this country. He painted the altars in numerous churches in Upper Austria and Bohemia, in addition to a number of portraits, such as the portrait of Count Thun, the Bishop of Passau. There was no technique he would not try out, including engravings and lithographs. He produced over 300 graphics of all types, mostly large compositions depicting allegorical, mythological, and biblical scenes, as well as portraits, new year's cards, and visiting cards, both of his own designed or inspired by old masters. His work used to be considered too academic and cold. As time went by, his critics began to reevaluate his work and eventually it found gratification. Today, it is highly recognized for its distinct characteristics: masterly routine, unaffectionate serenity, and meticulous precision.

Joseph Bergler ended up staying in Prague in the capacity of the Fine Arts Academy's director until his death in 1829. Over that period, he educated a whole pleiad of future Bohemian artists. Let us name a few of them: František Horčička (1776 - 1856), František Tkadlík (1786 - 1840), Joseph Navrátil (1798 - 1865), and sculptor Václav Prachner (1785 - 1832). Joseph Bergler - who was a son of a sculptor, after all - cooperated with sculptors frequently, both thematically and conceptually. In addition to the above mentioned Václav Prachner, he was also known to have worked with Josef Malinský (1752 - 1827), Václav Nedoma (1778 - 1833) and others.

An example of such a cooperation was the development of a former country estate of the Cibulka family in Prague-Košíře. After the dissolution of the Passau Principality in 1803, the estate was bought by Bishop Leopold Leonard, Count Thun-Hohenstein, who had notions of retiring there. Not only did he have the entire estate reconstructed to suit his needs and ideas, he also had landscape architects design an enormous English-style park, adorned with small romantic architectural elements and art works. Much use was made of the water element, too. The reconstruction of the estate involved all of the above named sculptors, whose creations were based on Joseph Bergler's drawings. No wonder that Count Thun-Hohenstein had so much confidence in Joseph Bergler - they had known each other very well from Passau. It is conceivable that Bergler was instrumental as an adviser in the design of the entire layout of the estate.

When Count Thun-Hohenstein died, on October 22, 1826, his nephew, Joseph Matthias Thun, had an exquisite monumental tombstone made, whose artistic significance was well ahead of its time. The author of the ornamental funeral sculpture was Václav Prachner, who followed sketches drawn by the director of the Academy of Fine Arts in Prague - namely, Joseph Bergler.

Around 1820, one of Bergler's students, František Nadorp, painted a portrait of Bergler. Today, the oil painting is property of the Museum of Metropolitan Prague. Another portrait of Bergler, a self-portrait, has also been preserved to this day. A fact of interest is that, in May 1820, Joseph Bergler was among the guests attending the christening of Joseph Mánes, the most prominent Bohemian painter of the century, at St. Hastal's Parish Church in Old Town Prague.

Joseph Bergler extended the original contract appointing him to the directorship of the Academy of Fine Arts in Prague several times. He died on June 25,1829, in Prague and is buried at the Olšany Cemetery II, 8th section, grave No. 69. He was succeeded by František Waldherr, his long-time assistant and a master drawer. Quite recently, in the beginning of 1995, the Academy of Fine Arts in Prague organized an exposition of a collection of historic drawings of its first director, Joseph Bergler. Also presented were master copies of the sketches which Bergler had at one time brought from Italy. These sketches happen to be the oldest artifacts deposited in Archives of the Academy of Fine Arts. The event was a dignified tribute to Bergler's merits and memory.

Prague - Hradčany and Malá Strana. Detail from *PRAGA BOHEMIA METROPOLIS ACCURATISSIME EXPRESSA 1592*; woodcut by J. Kozel and M. Peterle of Annaberg (?) in Prague (Vratislav - Municipal Library)

Tycho

BRAHE

O ne of the most outstanding personalities of Rudolfinian Prague was Tycho Brahe (1546 - 1601), a Danish astronomer. Fate had it that this world-famous scientist concluded his lifelong quest for stars in Prague, too, where he was ceremoniously buried at the Virgin Mary před Týnem Church on Staroměstské náměstí [Old Town Square]. The inquisitive tourist may view his tomb and a marble epitaph written on the adjoining column. Tour guides like to tell the story of his last moments over and over. During a festive dinner with the Emperor, where it was not allowed - under the rules of the etiquette - to stand up from the table before the Emperor did, the scientist held his urine for so long that his bladder burst. This is evidently nonsense, just as the claim that someone could commit suicide by holding his breath long enough is foolishness; nevertheless generation and generation of tourists is being served the story as if it were true. Legends of famous people sell very well. Besides, they are nice to listen to...

Tycho Brahe was born on December 14, 1546, at a farm

estate in Knudstrup. His original first name, Tyge, was later latinized to Tycho. His father, Otto Brahe, was of noble descent. Apart from Tycho and another boy who died, he and his wife, Beata, born Bille, had five other sons and the same number of daughters. Tycho Brahe studied at the Copenhagen University, specializing mainly on mathematics and astronomy. He was immensely impressed by the solar eclipse on Aug. 21, 1560, (total in Portugal and partial in Copenhagen), which astronomers had predicted. It may well have been the reason for his subsequent choice of scientific specialization.

He transferred to several European universities where he excelled in mathematical sciences and Latin, in particular. In 1566, he had an accident in Rostock in Holstein. Following an argument, on Dec. 10, with one of his countrymen, a Danish aristocrat named Manderup Parsbjerg, he got involved in a sword duel, in which he lost most of his nose. He had to have a prothesis made of gold and silver. For the rest of his life, he carried a jar with a salve he would smear on the artificial nose.

When his father died, on May 9, 1571, Tycho, being the eldest, took charge of the family estate. A year later, he married a daughter of a tenant farmer, Kristina, with whom he had eight children. Tycho Brahe continued his activities in astronomy. In 1575, for instance, when he did astronomical research at a local observatory in Kassel, staying with Count von Hessen, he met, for the first time, his future employer, the ruler of Bohemia, Rudolf II, and his personal doctor Tadeáš Hájek z Hájku, with whom he made a permanent friendship. In the same year, he returned to his homeland to become the court astronomer of King Fridrich II. The King had a magnificent observatory built for the scientist, on the Island Hveen, and a house for his family. The observatory, which Tycho Brahe named Uraniborg, became one of the main centers of astronomy in the 16th century. The astronomer, who was quite famous by then, lived a peaceful and content existence, especially after he was granted a fief on the island and all the serfs on it.

Everything changed after King Fridrich II died, on April 4, 1588. The royal court and even the crown prince himself, Prince Kristian, who was 11 at the time of the King's death, suddenly began to be bothered by the costs of the observatory's operation and acquisition of expensive instruments. First, Tycho Brahe sold his family estate in Knudstrup, but when the salary for his services as a royal astronomer was suspended and the royal fief to the island was cancelled, he interrupted his work and moved to Copenhagen with his family. Here, he waited for a change in the political climate, but in vain. Bitter and hurt, he left his native Denmark. At first he sought shelter in Rostock, Holstein, then in Wandsbeck, and finally in Wittenberg. To the latter mentioned location, he arrived in the winter 1598, not only with his family but also with some of his students.

It was here that he received the invitation from Emperor Rudolf II in Prague. It is known that the idea to invite him had been initiated by Tadeáš Hájek z Hájku (1525 - 1600), the Emperor's personal doctor and a genuine Renaissance man, i.e., a well-rounded man of many interests. Among other things, he was also interested in astronomy - in fact, one of the craters on the Moon is named after him: *Hagecius*. He was an equally proficient botanist - in 1562, he prepared the publication of the famous *Herbarium* by Matthioli. Moreover, he was a famous medicine man, literature connoisseur, and was in charge of the Emperor's alchemy workshop.

The Emperor received the world-famous astronomer with great honors and enthusiasm, overwhelming him with his favors. These included also an offer of top notch accomodations: a roomy Renaissance summer palace which used to belong to Jacob Kurz, where Tycho Brahe was to live upon arriving to Prague. The rooms in it were furnished in accordance with his wishes, as was his astronomical observatory. Rudolf II eventually purchased the summer palace for him as Jacob Kurz died in 1594, paying a handsome sum of 10,000 Imperial thalers for it - some sources claim that it was a double of that amount - to Jacob's widow, Anna Kurz. Thus, in addition to finding a fine position in Prague, Tycho Brahe gained a property of considerable value. It is depicted in a chronicle titled *Historia Coelestis*, published in 1672 in Regensburg. At that time, it was the highest-esteemed residence in Prague. Attached to the palace was a sizeable garden, as Tycho Brahe wrote in a letter to his brother-in-law, Holger Rosenkranz, inviting him to Prague for the wedding of his daughter Elizabeth. The house used to stand partly in the place of today's Johann Kepler High School and the open area near the Pohořelská tram stop. It was demolished sometime after the Thirty Years' War to make room for the construction of a new massive fortification of Prague. A 1901 search for fragments of the former summer palace was successful enough to locate some layout details and facilitate some photographic and sketch-book documentation.

A major affair in Rudolfinian Prague was Tycho Brahe's dispute with the Capuchin Order. The Capuchins came to Prague in 1599 at the request of the Prague Archbishop Berka z Dubé and Emperor Rudolf II, upon accepting the recommendation of the Trident Church Council. They were brought to Prague by Lorenzo of Brindisi, who was later sanctified. They built a church dedicated to the Virgin Mary and a monastery in the lower part of today's Loretánské náměstí (the latter still under construction at the time of the dispute). It was customary for the Capuchins to always ring the bells in a little tower, three times, whenever going to the choir gallery. This irritated the famous astronomer very much, for his observatory was nearby and it distracted him as he was concentrating on his stellar observation. The dispute turned into a crisis and had to be resolved by Emperor Rudolf II himself. Although he managed to quell the fiercest altercations; however, since the affair, in terms of its consequences, had turned into a confrontation of the Catholics and the Protestants, the matter could not be resolved to any satisfaction until the astronomer died in 1601.

One of Tycho Brahe's great merits was that he had offered support to his younger colleague, astronomer and mathematician Johann Kepler. To help his protégé, Brahe used the strong influence he had on the Emperor on Kepler's behalf. Kepler repaid the service by continuing in his master teacher's unfinished scientific work in Prague after Brahe died. Both men now have a monument in Pohořelec, created by the sculptor Josef Vajce. Its architectural concept had been prepared by Vladimír Pýcha, a Fine Arts Academy graduate. The monument was unveiled on July 20, 1984.

Tycho Brahe did some of his research in Benátky nad Jizerou, a town relatively close to Prague today. The reason was that the masters of Donín, owners of a Renaissance castle built by Bedřich of Donín before 1526, on the ruins of a former Gothic monastery, had gotten themselves into a financial crisis and were forced to sell the castle to Emperor Rudolf II. He then offered it to Tycho Brahe as an alternative residence and observatory. The Danish astronomer accepted the offer and set up permanent observatory stations in the castle's thirteen rooms, transporting and installing the necessary equipment there. His assistant in the astronomical activities was a Jewish scientist and astronomer, David Gans (1541 - 1613), whose tombstone, bearing a David star and a relief of a goose (the meaning of his surname in German), we find at the Old Jewish Cemetery in Prague.

The Danish astronomer Tycho Brahe had wanted to resettle with his entire numerous family to Bohemia, which he considered his second fatherland, but had not enough time left to carry out that intention. Falling gravely ill, he was delirious from a high fever for several days and, on October 24, 1601, he died in Prague. A most exquisite funeral was organized and held after almost two weeks, on November 4, attended by many secular and clerical dignitaries, family members, as well as the public. An interesting detail is that among the mourners in the funeral procession was also the astronomer's favorite horse. The obituary was read over the open tomb in the Týnský Chrám [Týn Cathedral] by Jan Jesenský of Jesenné, a medical doctor. Kristina, Tycho Brahe's widow, died in 1604 and was buried in the same vault, next to her husband.

In 1901, on the occasion of the 300th anniversary of Tycho Brahe's death, it was decided to subject the astronomer's remains to a thorough research examination and repair the vault and tombstone. At first, it was not certain whether both spouses were still there, because - after the White Mountain Battle and subsequent anti-reformist activities - non-Catholic corpses had been removed from the church. It turned out that this had not occurred in Brahe's case. The skeletal remains were thoroughly analyzed by experts from a Czech university, Prof. Dr. Ondřej Schrutz and Doc. Dr. Jindřich Matiegka. Among the finds were remnants of fabric and the astronomer's artificial nose. A detailed report of the exhumation was made, which confirmed, among other findings, that Tycho Brahe was indeed missing a part of his nose. Contrary to the myth about the cause of his death, the story about his nose is really true.

The skeletal remains were cleaned and put into new pewter coffin in the repaired vault. The reburial of Tycho Brahe and his wife Kristina was attended by: the main parish priest of Týnský Chrám, Dr. Eduard Knobloch, the first deputy mayor

JUDr. Vojtěch Frič, alderman Václav Brož, communal elder JUDr. Luboš Jeřábek, Prof. Ondřej Schrutz, M.D., director of the National Museum of Prague, Břetislav Jelínek, and Antonín Černý, an executive representative of the Society of Antique Dealers in Prague.

A German master (M. Wolgemut, W. Pleyden Wurff ?) the oldest view of Prague; woodcut from *Liber cronicarum*.
Dr. H. Schedel, Nuremberg 1493. (Prague - National Museum)

Johan

BROKOF

Of the sculptor workshops which existed at the beginning of the 18th century, Braun's and Brokof's stood out among the rest. Their masters, Matthias Bernard Braun and Ferdinand Maxmilian Brokof, created many magnificent pieces of art which we admire to this day. The founder of the Brokof family workshop was Johann Brokof (1652 - 1718). Johann Brokof was born on June 23, 1652, in Spišská Sobota, Slovakia, in the former Hungarian Empire. He was German, both from the paternal and maternal sides.
A carver an sculptor by trade, he left his birthplace for a reason which is stated in his letter of credence, dated 1675, "...to learn an honest trade."

Probably still in the same year, Johann Brokof arrived in Prague, where he worked for five years in a carver's workshop as a journeyman. He then spent two years on the estate of Count Matthias Wunschwitz von Ronsberg-Poběžovice in the area of Domažlice. During those two years, he made a model of the Charles Bridge, after a small clay model made by Matthias

Rauchmüller, a Viennese court sculptor. The model, carved out of wood, is a figure of a Bohemian favorite saint: Jan Nepomuk. In 1683, the sculpture of Jan Nepomuk was cast into bronze at the Nuremberg workshop of Jeronymus Herold. The bronze statue was placed on the Charles Bridge on August 31,1683. The very concept of the statue - the holy man is presented wearing a biret and loose garb, hanging down in folds, carrying a crucifix, a hallow of little stars over his head, which, according to a legend, had appeared over his dead body in the Vltava River - became a model for thousands of other Jan Nepomuk sculptures all over Bohemia and Moravia, and even elsewhere. Brokof's actual model remained in Wunschwitz's house in Prague - today it stands on the main altar of the St. Jan Nepomuk Church at Na Skalce in Prague. It remains to be added that Jan Nepomuk was blessed on May 31, 1721, and then ceremoniously sanctified on March 19, 1729.

A noteworthy detail certainly is that Johann Brokof, a Lutheran, converted to Catholicism while working on the Jan Nepomuk sculpture. He explains his reasons for doing so at length in a letter which was reprinted in 1895 in *Památky archeologické*. Among other things, he states: "Being a son of a Lutheran father and mother, I used to be so firm in my faith that no tearing of pieces of flesh from my body, day after day, could have shaken my conviction that I would be faithful to Lutheranism until the day I die". But in concluding his letter he writes: "But the aforementioned Baron (Matthias von Wunschwitz: authors' note) commissioned me to carve a sculpture of Jan Nepomuk, four ells tall, which was to be used for casting the statue, which now stands on a bridge in Prague, and - all of a sudden - during all the strain and diligence that I put into the work, a Holy Spirit's mercy enlightened me so that I - without any force whatsoever but of my own free will - took up reading Catholic books and realized that of all the faiths in the world only Christian Catholicism under St. Peter's guidance could lead to eternal salvation. And so, while working on the sculpture of Jan, I had a change of heart and turned away from heretical Lutheranism, converted to Catholicism in 1682 at Pivoni (an Augustinian monastery nearby : authors' note), for which decision I most gratefully and faithfully thank the Almighty God and St. Jan Nepomuk. Amen." He proved to have meant his conversion in the utmost seriousness sometime later when he tried to christen a Jewish boy, despite the protests of the boy's parents.

During the years 1683 - 1685, Johann Brokof worked in Manětín, where he left a number of wood sculptures of saints, e.g., St. Sigmund, Vitus, Norbert, Ivan, Anna, Elizabeth, Ludmila, and Eleanor at St. Barbara's Church, a local cemetery church. After crossing Klášterec nad Ohří and Červený Hrádek, he returned to Prague to settle down, establish a family workshop which was to become famous, especially through the merits of his son, Ferdinand Maxmilian Brokof.

On September 28, 1686, at the Virgin Mary před Týnem Church in Old Town Prague, Johann Brokof married Elizabeth Springer. The Book of Marriages identifies the best man as Vojtěch Pechr and that there were four witnesses: Jiří Kejha; Mrs. Kateřina Třebická, a woman of noble descent; Anna Ledvinka; and Johann Filip.

Three sons and one daughter were born from this marriage: Michael Johann Joseph Brokof (1686 - 1721), born in Klášterec, where his father worked on an assignment. Later, this son took over the family workshop for a short time. The most famous Brokof, Ferdinand Maxmilian (1688 - 1731), was born in Červený Hrádek. The daughter, Eleanor (1691 - 1741), was born in Bork and grew up to marry widower Filip Oberholtzer, a goldsmith in New Town Prague. The Brokofs' youngest son was born in 1693. Christened Antonín Sebastian, at the St. Henry's Parish Church in New Town Prague, this son did not follow the footsteps of his father and became a court poet and musician in Vienna.

The carver and sculptor Johann Brokof took Bohemian citizenship, with his children, on February 23, 1693, in Old Town Prague. On September 30 in the same year he bought a smallish house from Pavel Prosil, a tailor, on the corner of Uhelný Trh and Skořepka. The house, which no longer stands, bore number 421. Never short of work, Johann Brokof worked both in Prague and in numerous locations throughout the country. On the attic gable of the Tuscany Palace in Hradčany, there are seven of his sculptures, representing Seven Liberal Arts. In 1695, he won a commission to create a Piet, which stands at the Hospital pod Petřínem today. He participated in the creative decoration of a well-known pilgrimage spot at Svatá Hora [Holy Mountain] near Příbram, concretely, a so-called Prague Portal.

Of his works in the countryside, let us at least mention
Mary's Column on the town square in Broumov. The authorship
of the pieces made during the time when two of his sons, Michal
Johann Josef and Ferdinand Maxmilian, gradually began to join
him in the workshop, cannot be determined with certainty, even
though all of those sculptures and sculptural groups were
always signed with Johann Brokof's name.

Towards the end of his life, Johann Brokof had problems
with his house on Uhelný Trh No. 421. Since the courtyard in his
house was very small, Brokof would sculpt larger pieces
directly in front of his house - in the market square, actually.
This practice was going on much to the dismay of his neighbor,
the attorney-at-law Jiří Hoffmann. The lawyer reported Brokof
to the Mayor's Office and, on June 17, 1717, the city aldermen
determined that Brokof would not be able to carry out his trade
outside his property. Embittered, the artist sold his house and
bought another one, in the same year. His new house, called
U Salátků [Salatka's House] (not preserved to this day, either),
previously belonging to Sabina Barbara Schmidt, was situated in
New Town Prague. With much foresight, he anticipated that his
end was near, he left the property to his eldest son, Michal
Johann Joseph. Today, the place on Národní Třída, where
U Salátků used to be, is partly covered by an enormous four-
winged palace-like building No. 37, known as Jacob
Wimmer's House or also Porges von Portheim Palace.

The carver and sculptor Johann Brokof, upon receiving the
last rites, died of hydrops in his home. He was buried on
December 28, 1718, in the wall of the St. Martin's Church in Old
Town Prague. A large commemorative tablet of red marble with
a bronze plague by Josef Mařatka was placed there in 1909. The
plague also mentions that two of his sons are buried there as
well. Elizabeth Brokof survived not only her husband but also
both elder sons. She died at a high age of 80 years and was
buried on January 8, 1735.

Job. Wechter after Filip van den Bossche: Prague in 1606;
engraving 47.6 x 314 cm - detail from an engraving in
Graphische Ansichten von Prague 1498 - 1850 by Antonín
Novotný. Published in 1945 by V. Poláček, Prague

Enrico

CARUSO

T he Italian tenor, Enrico Caruso (1873 - 1921) is one of the
artists whose memory will forever be a part of the
treasury of opera stars. In his time, his star was
shining like a meteor on the most prominent boards of fame and
he also was one of the best paid opera singers in the world. In
1904, even the Prague audience had the opportunity to become
acquainted with the brilliance of his performance.

Enrico Caruso was born on February 27, 1873, in Naples, as
number 19, in his own words, for he was, indeed, the nineteenth
son of his parents, Marcel Caruso and his wife Anna, born
Baldini. Fate had been extremely cruel to them, for of all his
eighteen brothers died in their childhood. When Enrico was
three years old, the twentieth boy was born and soon thereafter
came Anna, the only daughter.

As a young boy, the future opera star had an extremely hard
life. He had to start working with his father in the factory to
help him provide for the family. The only person who believed
in Enrico's talent for singing and painting was his mother. With

her support, he sang, still as a school child, in the church choir, where he soon became a soloist. But his mother fell seriously ill and on July 1, 1888, she died. Thus the fifteen-year-old Enrico was half-orphaned. His father was a widower for only half a year, before he married Maria Castaldi - which was reportedly a happy decision, both for himself and the family.

Gradually, Caruso's talent was becoming more evident. As time went by, he stood out more and more among the voices in the choir and was frequently asked to sing for the guests of a nearby spa. But there was no money for him to study. To the benefit of Enrico and the world's opera scene, the young talent did get a chance to take lessons with a renowned voice teacher, Guglielmo Vergini, albeit under special conditions. The Master agreed to teach Caruso for free, if he promises to pay him one quarter of his revenues for five years if he were ever to successfully establish a career as a singer. You have guessed correctly, if you thought that the Master never regretted the contract thus conceived.

Caruso performed in an opera, for the first time, on the scene of a small theater, called Nuovo, in his native Naples. The name of opera was *Godfather Franz* and its premiere was held on November 16, 1894. The production of the opera as such was largely ignored by professional critics, nevertheless the few reviews that were written about it all praised Caruso's performance. Gradually, he would receive more and more offers to perform and his financial situation was improving. Eventually, Caruso was well off enough to be able to afford taking lessons with another teacher, Maestro Vincenco Lombardi. Thanks to diligence and perseverence, Caruso's star kept rising on the imaginary ladder of recognition and fame. He started to perform in different towns and went even to Cairo to sing. By 1897, he had eighteen operas in his repertoire.

More success came when he was cast for the role of Rudolph in Puccini's *La Boheme*, in which he triumphed. During August 1897 the opera was performed twenty-six times, always with Caruso singing the part of Rudolph. Another part in the same opera, the role of Mimi, was sung by Ada Giachetti, to whom Caruso felt a strong affiliation, not only artistically but also emotionally. As the affection was mutual, they moved together to Milan, without marrying. A son was born out of that relationship, whom they named Rudolph, in memory of

Caruso's first role and the time they met. Another child, illegitimate as well, was born in 1904. The young parents' expectation - that it would be a girl which they would name Mimi, after the mother's part in the Puccini's opera, naturally, was not to be fulfilled. It was not a crow that knocked on their window, but a stork, and everybody knows that storks bring only boys. Caruso's second-born son was given a name after his father, i.e., Enrico, but his parents called him Mimi for a long time anyway. But the duration of Caruso's happiness was measured. One day, upon returning home from a tour abroad, he did not find his common-law wife, Ada Giachetti, or sons, Rudolph and Enrico, in front of the fireplace. What he found instead was a letter telling him that he no longer meant anything to Ada as a man and that she was therefore leaving him forever. All Caruso's search for her and his children, even with the aid of private detective agencies, was fruitless and never saw her or the children again.

In the meantime, Caruso reached the climax of his career, when he became, in 1903, at the age of 30, a member of the Metropolitan Opera in New York. He presented himself to the applauding audience for the first time in the role of the duke in Verdi's *Rigoletto*. He stayed with the Metropolitan until 1920, when a fatal illness forced him to abandon his operatic career. During his engagement in New York, he frequently performed on the most prestigious scenes of the world, not only in America, but above all in Europe.

It was on one of those European tours, in 1904, that the phenomenal Italian tenor also came to visit Prague. Long before that visit, the two performance of Verdi's *Rigoletto* and Donizetti's *L'elisir d'amore*, two days thereafter, had been announced. In the former opera, Caruso sang the part of the Duke, in the latter, the part of Nemorino. The demand for tickets was tremendous - the performance was sold out to the last seat for both shows. Both performances were held on the stage of the then German Theater, the State Opera today. Much regret was expressed on the pages of the press over the fact that Caruso could not perform at the National Theater.

Caruso, who was accompanied to Prague by Arturo Vignas, a music conductor, as well as several singers, celebrated a huge success. Again and again, he would be called back on the stage for yet another encore by rapturous applause. For his extraordinary artistic performance, he received a huge quantity of flower bouquets. He gave thanks for each of them individually and, in an act of modesty, he would point to his co-performers, Pignataro, baritone, Arimondi, bass, and Mme. Pinkert, soprano. He also thanked the conductor, Artur Vignas, for his cooperation.

For his performance in Prague, Caruso arrived from Paris, where he had given a charity concert, the proceeds of which were to go to the benefit of the families of Russian soldiers who had fallen in the Russian - Japanese war. According to the contract, he then left for Dresden to appear, on May 8, as the Duke in *Rigoletto*. Due to a great interest of the public, he returned to the city of 100 spires on the Vltava River to repeat his successful performance on May 10-12, 1994.

Subsequently, he went to England where he performed at the London Royal Opera on May 19, 1904, in the role of Canio in Leoncavallo's *I Pagliacci* [The Comedians]. In the role of Neddy appeared, for the first time, an equally famous opera diva, Ema Destinnová, a native of Prague (1878 - 1930). From then on, the two stars formed an inseparable artistic pair on many boards of fame round the world, including the Metropolitan Opera in New York. It was here that Destinnová enraptured Caruso, especially on two occasions: for the first time, in her debut appearance as Aida on Nov. 16, 1908, and, for the second time, even more distinctly, on February 19 1909, during the first New York staging of Smetana's *Bartered Bride*, in the leading role of Mařenka. The opera was conducted by Gustav Mahler, a Czech composer and conductor, and choreographed by Otakar Bártík, another Czech, who was on engagement with the Metropolitan as a ballet maestro at that time. Caruso, in the company of Toscanini, a composer, followed the fantastic performance of Destinnová from a loggia and, completely enthralled, sent her a large bouquet of rare orchids on to the stage.

Caruso, being a first-ranking star, never was short of female admirers. His beautiful voice - it was rightfully claimed that he had a throat of gold - enchanted many a woman's heart. Women would shower not only flowers upon him, but also various gifts of gold and diamonds. In 1910, one of his female admirers even gave him an automobile. But Caruso was trying to win the heart of another woman - Ema Destinnová. As much as he tried, it was all in vain. The famous diva, well-known for her patriotic views and fervor for Bohemian causes, replied to his marriage proposal, when he finally found enough courage to ask, categorically: "If I ever get married, it will have to be a Czech." It is said that Caruso proposed in a covered coach as the two artists were returning from a concert to their hotel. Ema Destinnová repeatedly refused all suitors throughout her artistic career only to marry, towards the end of her life, Joseph Halsbach, an air force lieutenant and her junior by twenty years. She lived with him in a reportedly not very happy marriage until her death on Jan. 28, 1930.

On the other hand, it is documented that Caruso had spent the summer 1907 in the company of the opera diva at the castle Domousnice near Mladá Boleslav, where Destinnová spent her vacations. It is most likely that he repeated his visits in the summer 1911, when he took a leave of absence to recover from a most demanding operation on his vocal chords. According to Vladislav Mareš, a journalist with *Lidová Demokracie*, in an article dated November 5, 1992, the two famous stars had themselves photographed in Prague, at Langhans' studio, but the precious photographic plates have not been preserved. They were destroyed when the studio was expropriated and all its contents taken to the city dump. It is assumable that Caruso revisited Prague in the company of Ema Destinnová in 1911. An interesting detail is that hotel Palace, situated on the corner of Jindřišská and Panská Streets, built in 1906 in the style of Viennese Art Nouveau, has named one of its salons Enrico & Ema, in memory of both famous singers - but the early guest books of the hotel have not been preserved to date.

Towards the end of his starlit career, the famous Italian tenor, Enrico Caruso, did get married, after all. The woman of his choice was Dorothy Benjamin, 20 years his junior, whom he married on August 20, 1918. The happy couple barely managed to have a child, a daughter named Gloria, when it became evident that Caruso's candle of life was burning out. Befallen by a fatal illness, the singer appeared for the last time in Halévy's *The Jewess*, on December 24, 1920, at the Metropolitan Opera. He died on August 2, 1921, in his native Naples. Thanks to his thriftiness and kingly revenues - for he was paid as much as 10,000 dollars per night - he left his young widow a fairy-tale wealth. His body was embalmed and exhibited some time later in a glass coffin in Caruso's memorial.

Job. Wechter after Filip van den Bossche: Prague in 1606;
engraving 47.6 x 314 cm - detail from an engraving in *Graphische
Ansichten von Prague 1498 - 1850* by Antonín Novotný. Published
in 1945 by V. Poláček, Prague. A View of Ruine Castle Vyšehrad

Fryderyk (Fréderic)

CHOPIN

O n the corner of Na Příkopě and Senovážná Streets, we find a modern building No. 860 and 864, in which Státní banka [State Bank] is situated today. On this spot, there used to stand one of the renowned hotels of Prague, hotel *U Modré hvězdy* [Blue Star Inn]. Over its long existence, many distinguished visitors to Prague had stayed in it. The Polish music composer and piano virtuoso, Fryderyk Chopin (1810 - 1849) was one of them. On October 17, 1960, to honor his memory on the occasion of the 150th anniversary of his birth, a bronze commemorative plaque was unveiled, with a relief en face, created by woman sculptor, Marie Duras, a student of Jan Štursa. The text on it states: "Fryderyk Chopin, Polish music composer, lived in 1829 - 1830 in a house that used to stand in this place."

Fryderyk Chopin was born on February 22, 1810, in a town called Želazowa Wola, not far from Warsaw. His father, Nicolas Chopin, was of a French descent from Nancy, France, and his mother Justyna, born Krzyzanowska, was a Polish native. The couple married in 1806, and, apart from son Fryderyk, also brought up two daughters, Luisa and Isabela. Shortly after the couple's wedding, Nicolas Chopin became a professor at a high school and military schools in the capital city of Warsaw. In 1815, he opened a private boarding school for boys from affluent families, where he also taught several subjects, especially French. Both parents had a strong relationship to music; in addition to playing instruments, the mother also was a professional dancer. It was not hard for them to be recognize that their son was a musical prodigy.

The music teacher of young Fryderyk, and his sisters as well, was a Czech, Vojtěch Živný (1756-1842). Later on, around 1817, he became a full-time employee of Nicolas Chopin, but, as time went by, he was virtually considered a member of the family. Despite a great different in age, he became his student Fryderyk's very close friend. Their friendship, well documented in the form of preserved correspondence, lasted throughout their lives. In many publications on the history of European music it is stated that Fryderyk got his basic education in the piano and composition from a Czech named Vojtěch Živný. His grateful student composed, at the age of eleven, *Piano Polonaise As-major*, on which he wrote a dedication to his teacher.

The gifted boy was invited to all the aristocratic palaces where he enthused everyone with his brilliant play. Eventually he found another teacher, the director of the music conservatory, Joseph Elsner. Fully aware of the prodigiousness of his student, he never imposed any limits on his Fryderyk, giving his a great deal of creative freedom. In 1825, at the age of 15, Chopin performed for the Russian Czar Alexander. Impressed. the Czar showed his appreciation by giving him a diamond ring. In the same year, Chopin's first work, *Rondo in C-minor*, was published. He had written several compositions before, but they are preserved as manuscripts only. Four years later, two world-famous virtuosos came to Warsaw to give a concert: the first one was Hummel, a pianist and composer of Bratislava, and the second one was Paganini, a highly recognized "wizard on the fiddle". Young Chopin was enthralled by their play, but was also so impressed by their international renomé, which followed both artists wherever they went, that he decided he would also test his skills abroad. He left for Vienna, where he performed, on August 11 and 18, 1829, at the

Imperial Theater, with great success. The gate leading to
a triumphal road towards admiration and recognition had thus
opened before him.

From Vienna, Chopin, accompanied by his friends, Ignatius
Maciejowski and Alphons Brandt, went to Prague. He carried
a number of letters of recommendation from his Viennese fans.
Taking the express coach, they managed to make the trip from
Vienna to Prague in two nights and one day. Chopin wrote to his
parents from Prague, describing the journey as a pleasant one,
thanks to his nice companions. Upon arriving to Prague at noon,
Chopin found accommodations right away. After lunch he went
for a walk, with his friends, to the Prague Castle and St. Vitus
Cathedral, where he was most impressed by the St. Wenceslaus
Chapel, in particular. He was overwhelmed by the view from the
castle hill over the city. That's how it happened that they went
off schedule and did not have time enough left to do the next
point on their agenda - a visit with Václav Hanka (1791 - 1861),
a Bohemian poet, philologist, and member of the National
Enlightenment Movement.

Few and sporadic details are known about this three-day
visit of Fryderyk Chopin in Prague. The best source of
information are letters to his parents, with whom he shared his
impressions of the 100-spired city that lay on the Vltava River,
and about the social contacts he made. On the second day in
Prague, he and his friends caught up with their plan and visited
Václav Hanka, who was at that time one of the leading
advocates of Panslavic ideas. They met with him at his work
place, actually, i.e., the library of the Bohemian Patriotic
Museum Society - the National Museum today. The meeting
passed in a very amicable atmosphere and, before parting, the
young Poles were asked to make an entry in the guest book of
the Bohemian Museum. A mere signature would not do for
these talented men: one of them composed a short poem,
another one a piece of prose. Chopin, not wishing to be
outdone, asked Maciejowski to quickly write four stanzas of
a mazurka and then he put them into music. Hanka was thrilled,
for the mazurka was dedicated to him, i.e., to his merits in the
Slavic cause. He rewarded Chopin and his friends by acting as
their most enlightened guide around Prague for the rest of their
stay, telling them at length about the history of Prague and its
monumental places.

But when offered to give at least one public concert in Prague, Chopin categorically refused to accept. He declared - as he explains in a letter to his parents - that he did not wish to lose in Prague what he had won by his performances in Vienna, pointing out the circumstance that Pragonians were so sophisticated that even such a Maestro on the violin as Niccolo Paganini had not been received without some criticism. He would have probably accepted an offer to give a private concert, as he was giving preference to such concerts all his life, but he was not asked for one just then.

Fryderyk Chopin had some social obligations to carry out in Prague, too. He visited professor Bedřich Vilém Pixis (1786-1842), a violin teacher, conductor at Stavovské Theater, and a music composer, at the music conservatory in Řetězová Street in Old Town Prague. Upon handing to him the letters of recommendation from Vienna, we was cordially received. Pixis even interrupted his class to devote time to Chopin. During his next visit at Pixis' place, still the same day in the afternoon, Chopin met, at his own request, with a German pianist and organ player, Alexander August Klengel (1783 - 1852). For two hours Chopin and his friends sat and listened to him playing his Fugues. Chopin left Prague on the last day of his schedule, taking a rental coach at noon, arriving at Teplice in the evening. There he was asked to give a private concert at the Clary Castle and he obliged.

Chopin visited Prague for the second and last time in the Fall of 1830. Arriving on November 20, he stopped in Prague for one short day, again spending the night at the hotel *U Modré hvězdy* on his way from Dresden to Vienna. This second time, he did not perform in Prague either. Thus Chopin became one of the very few top concert masters of the time, whom the music-loving Pragonians never heard play.

Chopin parted with his native Poland, for good, on December 1, 1830. A concert and ceremonial banquet were organized in his honor. The Maestro also received a chalice filled with earth from his home country. Due to the war and political situation prevailing in Poland, he never returned. After a short stay in Vienna, where he made a close friendship with a Bohemian virtuoso violinist, Joseph Slavík, he left for Paris. He gave the first performance there on January 26, 1832, and gradually won so much fame and recognition that he became known all over France as the master of piano poetry. France became his new home.

In private life, Chopin did not have much luck. Although he knew many beautiful and well-educated young women, none of the relationships ended in a marriage. For a period of several years he maintained an affectionate - and perhaps intimate - relationship with a French female writer, George Sand, civil name Aurore Dupin. Despite great differences in their characters, Chopin found a lot of support in Sand as a woman who understood his music. Sand also did her best to protect Chopin's fragile health from getting any worse. It is believed that without her thoughtful care, his life would have been much shorter than it actually was. Chopin maintained relations with his parents through correspondence only - but he met with them many years later during his convalescence stay in Karlovy Vary [Carlsbad].

In the history of musical arts, Chopin is regarded as a leading representative of the era of Romanticism. His piano compositions number about seventy. Very popular to this day are especially his mazurkas, of which he composed 51 in all, in addition to waltzes and polonaises. Fryderyk Chopin died of tuberculosis, still a relatively young man, on October 17, 1849. Before he died, he wrote in his testament: "Since I am bound to suffocate under the weight of this earth, I adjure that my body be opened so I would not be buried alive." Upon taking his death mask, his wish was fulfilled. An autopsy was performed, his heart taken out and laid at rest at the Holy Cross Cathedral in Warsaw. In a grandiose funeral, Chopin's bodily remains were buried at the Pre Lachaise Cemetery in Paris. The handful of earth from his native land, which he had been given by his friends on his departure from Poland, was tossed onto his grave.

Václav Hollar: Prague 1636 or 1649; engraving from
Topographia Bohemiae, Moraviae et Silasiae by M. Zeiler,
Frankfurt am Main. Published in 1945 by V. Poláček, Prague

Ernest

DENIS

The French philosopher, historian, and Slavicist, great friend of the Czech nation and connoisseur of its precarious history, Ernest Denis (1849 - 1921) was born on January 4, 1849, in Nîmes, a town infamous for its fierce religious disputes and battles between its Catholic and Calvinist inhabitants. Denis hailed from a Calvinist family. Upon completing grammar school and graduating from the renowned and prestigious Ecole Normale Supérieure in Paris, he became a teacher in Corsica.

During the Franco-Prussian War, he had himself enlisted, without any hesitation whatsoever, in defense of Paris. His own words on the experience were: "On January 27, 1870, our battalion camped in Paris on Boulevard Richard-Lenoir. We knew that Jules Favre had returned from Versailles, where he had signed the capitulation of Paris. Shooting was now heard only at long intervals in the suburbs of Paris. With a deadly anxiety we awaited the moment when the cannonade would die down completely. All of a sudden, our captain started to weep and many of us wept with him. 'Why are you crying?', he said to us. 'You are young and will live long enough to see our victory over the Germans'."

To young Denis, the Bohemian Manifest of December 8, 1870, was like a salve for the soul. Initiated by Dr. František Ladislav Rieger, this courageous, isolated protest was proof of the small Bohemian nation's solidarity with the French against Prussian malice. Perhaps, putting it simply, this had awakened Denis' interest in a tiny country in Central Europe.

Thanks to his extraordinary academic aptitude and diligence, the young historian, Denis, was awarded a scholarship by the French Ministry of Education to study Bohemian history, language, and literature in Prague. He arrived in Prague in November of 1872 and found suitable lodgings with the family of a well-known painter and professor of drawing and graphic arts at a Municipal Girls College, Soběslav Hippolit Pinkas (1827 - 1901). They had met at the recommendation of Louis Leger (1843 - 1923), who felt very attached to the people of Bohemia, as his fourteen visits to the country testify. Among his friends also were František Palacký, František Ladislav Rieger, Julius Grégr, and Jan Neruda. Louis Leger was very interested in the Bohemian cause and sympathized with the Bohemian struggle for national identity. Pinkas met Leger during one of his frequent trips to Paris. Members of a very old Prague family, both the grandfather and father Pinkas were prominent Prague attorneys and political activists - Denis must have felt very much at home in their company. Conversation was not only in Czech but also in French, as Soběslav Pinkas had met his wife in France and brought her to Bohemia. Besides, his two daughters were both born in France. At the Pinkas'house, Denis made a pledge - which he fulfilled completely - that he would devote his professional life above all to Bohemian history.

Denis studied Czech with the poet Jaroslav Vrchlický, who commented with satisfaction that it helped him improve his French considerably. Denis was also interested in the history and languages of other Slavic nations and therefore extended his language lessons to Russian, with Professor Dr. Řeřábek, and Bulgarian, with K. Jireček.

Prague made a profound impression on him. With much interest, he focused primarily on ancient antagonisms between the Slavic and Germanic worlds. For these purposes, Prague's libraries and archives provided him with ample research opportunities.

As his major specialization, Ernest Denis concentrated on *Mistr Jan Hus* and the Hussite Uprising. However, to successfully dedicate oneself to history in Prague, would necessitate getting as close as possible to historiographer František Palacký.

Denis was introduced to him by the aforementioned promoter of Bohemian - French relations, Louis Leger. Palacký showed a great deal of understanding for and interest in his young colleague, entrusting to him his recently compiled collection of sources on the Hussite era in Bohemia. Later on, Denis' translator, Prof. Jindřich Vančura, wrote: "The great expectations which Palacký laid on the shoulders of this young historian were surpassed."

In order to be able to study primary historic sources on his own, Denis learned also German and Polish. Soon enough, he published his first minor writings, among them *Počátky Jednoty bratrské* [The Beginnings of Brotherly Unity] and *Jiří z Poděbrad*. In 1878, his first more extensive publication followed, titled *Hus and Hussite Wars*, in which he presented Hussitism as a religious movement based on old national traditions. He also presented this work at the Sorbonne in Paris as his dissertation thesis, which he successfully defended, and for which he was awarded a doctorate. Of his other publications, the most outstanding is *The End of Bohemian Independence* and, above all, his masterwork, *Bohemia After the White Mountain Battle*. In the latter work, Denis had elaborated on historic material which had previously not been extensively researched; the information available on the topic had been limited to incomplete research attempts of his predecessors. For that, his thoroughly researched work deserved even more praise.

After returning to France, Denis became a professor of history at the university in Grenoble, then in Bordeaux. As has been mentioned, for his scientific research on Jan Hus and the Hussite Wars, he had earned a doctoral degree and, in 1879, he became an associate professor at a university in Paris. Finally financially secure, in 1882 he married the daughter of his university colleague, Prof. Friedel. His marriage was very harmonious and endowed with several children. Unfortunately, his son fell during WW I, in 1915, in Loraine, France.

In 1912, a great parade was organized in Prague, where, on July 1, a monument of František Palacký (1798 - 1876), created by the sculptor Stanislav Suchard, was to be unveiled. The main speakers at the event were JUDr. Karel Groš, the Mayor of the royal capital city of Prague, and JUDr. Karel Kramář, a member of the Parliament. Ernest Denis, who arrived from Paris to attend the event, gave a short speech as well.

The French historian actively participated in the independence struggle of the Bohemian nation. During the decisive moments, after 1910, he turned from a historian into a politician - a politician who had much weight, for he had all the necessary knowledge of historic background of the situation. His advice to the Bohemian underground movement after the outbreak of WW I was: "You must not miss the right moment for overthrowing the Hapsburgs. You will never get another chance like this again." He also helped the Czechs in exile: at one point he lent them as much as 20,000 FF, a considerable amount of money. Moreover, his house on Rue Michelet became something like a Czechoslovak embassy in Paris. He also helped with publications and the distribution of news about the Bohemian cause in exile. His contribution to the independence of Czechoslovakia was noted even by T. G. Masaryk, the first president of the Republic.

Ernest Denis visited Prague for the last time in November 1920 to personally express his joy over the successfully developing Czechoslovak state. The cold autumn weather caused his to fall ill and he had to be hospitalized in the Podol Sanatorium. On departure, he said he felt that the time has come for Prague to once again assume the position it held during the reign of Charles IV, i.e., in the foreground of the Slavic nations. Upon his return from Prague, he celebrated his 72nd birthday and, two days thereafter, on January 5, 1921, he died.

In recognition and honor to Prof. Ernest Denis' contribution to the Bohemian nation, the ties he had felt to the country, his true friendship, inseparable and faithful, and his knowledge of old historic Prague, the *Klub Za starou Prahu* [Club for Old Prague] voted him, unanimously, an honorable member of the Club. It is the highest honor the Club can give. The letter of appointment is dated May 11, 1919, and bears the signatures of Eustach Mölzer, chairman, Eduard Schwarzer, deputy chairman, and Jan Almer, director.

On the occasion of the 10th anniversary of the foundation of Czechoslovakia, a monument was built to commemorate Ernest Denis, and ceremoniously unveiled, on October 27, 1928, in the lower part of Malostranské náměstí in Prague. The act represented not only a tribute to the great French scholar, but also, in a broader sense, a symbol of Czech - French friendship. The designer of the monument was Antonín Dvořák, a professional sculptor, who had won a public tender before being commissioned to do the work.

The ceremonial unveiling of the monument was also attended by President T. G. Masaryk, members of the Parliament and National Assembly, a French delegation, the diplomatic corps in Prague, and many prominent guests, as well as the general public. The ceremony was opened with the Czechoslovak state anthem and - as the monument was being unveiled - the Marseillaise. The main speaker was the minister of external affairs a future president of the Czechoslovak Republic, Edvard Beneš. In conclusion, the Hlahol Choir sang a eulogy song: *Sláva Tobě, velký Slávy synu* [Glory to you, son of Glory].

During the German occupation of Prague, Denis' monument was destroyed. The *Národní Politika* daily of April 23, 1940, printed a brief note of it from the Czech Press Agency, as follows: "Denis' monument for war purposes. Both mayors (Czech and German: authors' note) of the capital city of Prague have decided to remove Denis' monument on Malostranské náměstí. The monument was removed in the night on Monday and sent to the foundry for smelting."

Prague's inhabitants, unfortunately, got another reminder of Denis in connection with a similar act of vandalism many year later. It happened on March 15, 1985, when the authorities in power ordered a completely unfounded and unnecessary demolition of the historically and architecturally precious Praha-Těšnov Railway Station. Old Pragonians recall very well that between the World Wars the station used to be called *Denisovo*. Under German occupation, its official name was Prag Moldaubahnhof - Praha Vltavské nádraží, to be definitely renamed under the Communist regime in 1950.

Job. Wechter after Filip van den Bossche: Prague in 1606;
engraving 47.6 x 314 cm - detail from an engraving in *Graphische
Ansichten von Prague 1498 - 1850* by Antonín Novotný.
Published in 1945 by V. Poláček, Prague. A View of Karlov

Thomas Alva

EDISON

O ne of the world's most famous innovators, Thomas
Alva Edison, the pioneer of universal utilization of
electrical energy, was born in the small hours on
February 11, 1847, in a town called Milan, Ohio. The Edison
family did not have a luxurious station, so the life of the
technical genius and world-famous businessman was very
hard at first.

He attended school for only three months out a the year,
because his teacher complained that he was feebleminded; his
mother, Nancy Edison, took up teaching him at home. When
he was young, he sold vegetables and newspapers, and later
became a journalist and telegrapher. He learned telegraphing
from the station master, J. V. Mackenzie, in a small town
called Mount Clemens, as a small reward for saving a two-
year-old from being crushed under the wheels of a passing
locomotive.

Edison, who all his life had to cope with a partial handicap
in the form of poor hearing, was an extraordinarily diligent

student and was always busy experimenting with something. In those days, it was still quite common to regard such people as engaged in the "black arts". The first patent registered in his name bears the date June 1, 1869; it was an automatic electrical counter of votes in legislative committees. It did not earn him much success, but the invention was followed by an incredible number - at least 1,500 - of patents, mostly in the field of electrotechnology. They brought him not only fame and money, but also immortality. In general, it can be said that Edison's inventions set off a new era for mankind: the electricity era.

In 1888, a gifted young man offered his services to the great American innovator; he was Emil Kolben (1862 - 1943), a graduate of the Czech Technical University and later on a prominent entrepreneur. As a reward for excellent academic results, he had been granted Gerstner's scholarship. The offer was accepted and Kolben, who was taking a tour of the United States, appeared for work at Edison's place. At first, he worked in Edison's factory, the *Edison Machine Company*, for a starting salary of 15 dollars per week, but later on he became Edison's assistant in his research laboratory in Orange, which featured a scientific library with an incredible 60,000 volumes of books. Since Kolben proved to be very useful, he was promoted to the position of a chief engineer and put in charge of all the engineering offices and research labs of the Edison General Electric Company in Shenectady. Sometime later, back in his native Bohemia, he liked to recall some of Edison's statements. For instance, the statement that a completed invention is one per cent inspiration and ninety nine per cent hard work, or another statement claiming that four hours of sleep a day were enough and anything else was an indecent luxury.

Experience acquired during his stay in the United States served Emil Kolben very well upon his return home and lead to the foundation of a world-famous company *Českomoravská Kolben-Daněk*, which produced locomotives, turbo-compressors, etc. And it was Kolben who invited Thomas Alva Edison to Prague during Edison's tour of Europe. Before coming to see the 100-spired city of Prague, the great innovator, accompanied by a number of companions, including his second wife, twenty-year-old daughter, and thirteen-year-old son, went to visit Brno. He viewed the various points of interest, including the Brno City Theater electrically lit according to Edison's electrical-circuit scheme.

Edison started his four-day stay in Prague on September 13, 1911. He was staying in a then very prestigious, no longer existing, hotel *U Saského dvora*, called *Hotel de Saxe* for short, in Hybernská Street. The hotel, which used to stand across from the former Hybernian monastery, was famous, among other things, for its association with other famous guests, e.g., the music composer Peter Ilich Tchaikovsky and German writer Karel May.

During his motorized tour of Prague, Edison was accompanied by, besides from Emil Kolben, the American Consul. Reportedly, the great American innovator's first visit was paid to Café Edison situated on the corner of Václavské náměstí [Wenceslaus Square] and Na Můstku [On the Bridge]. He was received by Mr. Turnovský, the owner of the Café himself. When asked about the origin of this unusual name, he explained readily: The location was the meeting point of two promenades, the Czech and the German. If the Café had a German name, no Czech would come there, and vice versa. Therefore, he named his Café after a popular personality abroad so as not to offend anyone. The unusual name caught on and helped make his enterprise attractive to all. Satisfied with this explanation, Edison said: "Your words please me very much, because you were right to assume that I want to serve all the nations in the world equally, for the results of my work belong to all." Since it was a rainy day, Edison spent a good time in the Café with Kolben. Sitting at the with a view of Václavské náměstí, Emil Kolben told his guest stories about the memorable moments of this well-known Prague boulevard. The entrepreneur Turnovský made use of the opportunity and asked his guest to write a note in the guest book for the occasion of his visit. Edison obliged and Turnovský had the page framed and hung it up over the table where Edison had been sitting. It was the best advertisement he could possibly get for his business.

Edison was later received at the Old Town City Hall by the Mayor of Prague then in office, JUDr. Karel Groš, and there, too, he put an inscription in the guest book. He was presented

with a book of Prague and asked the Mayor for his autograph.
It is no wonder that, during the tour of the City Hall, Edison
was most fascinated by the complex mechanism of the
medieval horologe - Pražský orloj.

He then went to see the Prague Castle and the still
unfinished St. Vitus Cathedral. He also visited Zlatá ulička
[Golden Street] and Daliborka [Dalibor's Tower]. Next he
honored with his visit the Premonstrate monastery on
Strahov, where he admired the electrical lighting of the main
altar in the St. Rochus Church.

Edison also visited his Czech colleague by profession, the
electrotechnician and innovator František Křižík, at his
factory in Karlín, where he examined with much interest the
individual operations. The two men had much in common
- far more than the same year of birth - 1847. Both of them had
started with the telegraph, both of them had worked on
electricity, and both of them had put electrical energy to work
in transportation. Edison had experimented with electrical
locomotives as far back as 1880 in Menlo Park. Křižík had
built his first electrical tramway in Prague on the occasion of
the World Jubilee Exposition in 1891. Its tracks went from
Letná to Královská obora. In 1905, he built an electrical
railway from Tábor to Bechyně. The two gentlemen, who both
promoted the direct-current system, must have had much to
talk about.

The American innovator found even time to visit house No.
180, *U Modré štiky* [Blue Pike], in Old Town Prague. This was
where Dismas Šlampor, alias Viktor Ponrepo, was operating
a „biograph". Hearing that this was the first movie theater in
Prague, Edison spent over half an hour there. On leaving, he
tapped the surprised owner on the shoulder and said : "It is
small, but very good. It's what a movie house should look like."

The contemporary press did not pay much attention to
Edison's visit. Of the journalists in Prague, young Ervín Kisch
was the only one who made an interview with him. From it
the Prague paper's readers learned, among other things, that
the American innovator slept very little, ate modestly, did not
drink alcohol, but enjoyed an occasional cigar. In his
interview, Edison mentioned the longevity in his family. His
father lived to the age of 98 and died of a fall from the stairs;
his grandfather died at 102.

On September 22, 1911, the *Zlatá Praha* magazine printed the following piece of news: "Thomas Alva Edison, famous American innovator, a man whose name will forever be connected with the history of technical progress in the 19th century, thanks to his overwhelming conquering of electrical power and its epochal application in the services of the telegraph, telephone, lighting, and propelling etc., visited Prague for several days during his grand tour of Europe. He viewed several electrotechnical enterprises and points of interest in Prague, speaking favorably of the beauty of Prague and the wealth of its monumental places." The article also featured a photograph showing Edison in an automobile during his tour of Prague.

From Prague Edison went to visit some of the great cities of Germany, namely, Dresden, Berlin, and Nuremberg. Shortly thereafter, the newspaper printed another brief message stating that during Edison's trip through the last named city, there had been an accident. One of the automobiles (in Edison's motorcade) inadvertently ran over a twelve-year-old boy who died on the spot.

The advocate of work and the symbol of progress, innovator Thomas Alva Edison, died at an advanced age of 85 years on October 18, 1931, at his house in Menlo Park. His departure was mourned by the whole world. A following telegram of sympathy was sent to the President of the United States of America, Herbert C. Hoover, from so far away as Czechoslovakia. The text of the telegram was: "With much anxiety and tension, Czechoslovakia followed the last struggle of Thomas Alva Edison. Please accept our sincere sympathy over the loss of this man of gigantic spirit. Born and lived to become a part of our souls, Edison shall continue to be an eternal symbol of technical development in the modern era and its greatest advocate forever." The telegram, sent on October 19, 1931, from Prague, was signed by the President of the Czechoslovak Republic, T.G. Masaryk.

Folpertus van Ouden-Allen: Prague in 1685 with Malá Strana, engraving. Published in 1945 by V. Poláček, Prague

Albert

EINSTEIN

A mong the many foreigners who stayed in Prague for short or extended periods of time was also the ingenious German physicist, Albert Einstein (1879 - 1955), the discoverer of the theory of relativity, and scientist, whose formula $E = mc^2$ turned the accepted views on the world and space upside down and backwards. Let us mention right from start that Einstein spent time in Prague in 1911 - 1912, on an assignment, essentially, for he was serving during that time as a regular professor at the German University of Prague, simultaneously acting as the head of the Institute of Theoretical Physics, Prague.

Albert Einstein was born on March 14, 1879, in Ulm in southern Germany. Until 1894, he studied at the high school in Munich, which he left one year before graduating. He continued his studies on an individual basis, simultaneously attending a cantonal school in Zurich. Although he was not even 18 years old, he was granted an exception, thanks to his exceptional talent, and was admitted to the prestigious Confederation

Technical University in Zurich. The University's four-year curriculum specialized in the preparation of future teachers of natural sciences and mathematics.

One of Einstein's student colleagues was a young woman of Serbian descent, Mileva Marič (1875 - 1947), a very gifted and ambitious girl. That University was one of the few institutions which accepted female students. The young pair, though Mileva was Einstein's senior by a few years, attended the same lectures, eventually finding much liking for each other. Another common interest they had was music. At first, marriage was out of the question. Both of them had very high ambitions in science and quite definite ideas of their futures. But in the beginning of 1902, Mileva gave birth to a girl and her dream of an independent career in science began to dwindle. She put little Lizie into foster care - for good, as it turned out later (some sources claim that the girl had been adopted), but at the same time she suppressed her ambition in science and decided to accept Einstein's marriage proposal, despite her parents' disapproval. They married, against the will of both their parents, in January 1903.

Another child - legitimate, this time - was born to the couple, Mileva and Albert Einstein, in May 1904. It was a boy named Hans Albert. Both parents worked in science as much as they could. Historians cannot agree to this day, what share Einstein's wife may have had in his scientific discoveries and scientific publishing. But the ingenious physicist was an intellectual hermit at heart and after a few years of marital bliss he began to detest the institute of marriage and the presence of children. We speak in the plural, because in 1910 the Einsteins had another son, who was named Edward. However, this son was a very sickly child right from the time he was born and required constant care. This was shortly before Einstein's assignment to Prague.

In 1910, the German University in Prague had a vacancy for a professor of physics, since professor Ferdinand Lippich was retiring. Let us mention that his retirement was much deserved as he had been teaching at the school since 1874. The Commission of Competence recommended - to the Ministry of Culture and Education in Vienna - that the position be offered to Albert Einstein, who was at that time teaching at a technical school in Zurich, Switzerland, and was very interested in Prague. Einstein was finally chosen for the position, out of three other candidates, and Emperor Franz Joseph I himself confirmed his acceptance by signing the letter of appointment on January 6, 1911, effective as of April 1, 1911. Thus Einstein became full professor of theoretical physics at the German University in Prague.

The ingenious scientist arrived in Prague with his whole family: his wife Mileva, and two sons, Hans Albert (7) and Edward (1), as well as his mother-in-law, Maria Marič. They moved into house No. 1215/7 in Smíchov, on Třebízského Street, which is Lesnická Street today. The house had been newly built and the Einsteins lived in a relatively comfortable three-bedroom apartment on the 4th floor. The surrounding buildings were all new, as well; most of their inhabitants were senior officers, scientists, and artists. The proximity of the Vltava River where the family could take walks along the shore was certainly very pleasant. The Smíchov House No. 1215 bears a commemorative plaque with Einstein's bust and the following text: "In the years 1911 - 1912, Albert Einstein lived and worked in this house."

From the apartment in today's Lesnická Street, Einstein had only a short walking distance to his pedagogical and scientific work place in today's building No. 159/7 on Viničná Street, which belongs to the Faculty of Natural Sciences of Charles University. The distance was just right for a pleasant daily walk. He would cross Palacký bridge, walk through the Na Moráni Street, past *Faust's house*, and in a few more minutes he was in Viničná Street.

His study was on the 2nd floor and the auditorium where he gave lectures was on the ground floor. Not many student registered for his lectured, which was accountable to the fact that enrollment in the German University in Prague was very low. It is said that Einstein assured his students that they could interrupt him any time and ask a question, if they needed an explanation in something.

During his stay in Prague, Einstein not only lectured, but also continued in his scientific activities. He wrote about 15 theoretical papers of various lengths, among them - as he mentions in his biography - an article of the influence of gravitation fields on the distribution of light or an article on the consequences of the theory of relativity on the shifting of spectral rays towards the red end of the gravitation field. In connection with his work, he would highly praise the choice of sources at the Faculty's library. Today's visitor to the Faculty of Natural Sciences finds in the entrance hall a conspicuous commemorative plaque. The plaque features a likeness of the world-famous scientist and the following text: "In 1911 - 1912, Albert Einstein (1879 - 1955) worked as a professor in this building." Without any doubt, many an institution would be proud to have a plaque like this one. For precision's sake, let us also mention that Einstein's stay in Prague was frequently interrupted as he traveled to various international science symposia.

In addition to teaching at the Faculty of Natural Sciences, Einstein also lectured at the Klementinum in Old Town Prague, today's Slavic Library. His lectures here found a considerably larger audience. To the Klementinum, too, he would walk from his Smíchov apartment, a little way along Vltava, crossing Kampa, and Karlův most [Charles Bridge]. He loved the historical aspects of Prague. In his letter dated May 13, 1911, he confides to his friend, Michel Bess: "Prague is wonderful, it is so beautiful it would justify living here a lot longer." What he did not like in Prague was the polluted air in it, yes, even then. But he lived in Smíchov, i.e., the part of Prague which industrialization took by storm. He also had reservations about the quality of the drinking water in Prague, complaining that it was undrinkable, unless boiled first.

Although Einstein was a rather introverted man, as the case among top scientists often is, he did participate in Prague's cultural life. During rare moments of leisure he would join the philosophical or literary round tables which used to meet at Louvre Café on Národní třída. Occasionally, he was a guest in the salon of Mrs. Berta Fanta, wife of the owner of the pharmacy *U jednorožce* [Unicorn] in house No. 550, called *U Kamenného stolu* [Stone Table], at Staroměstské náměstí [Old Town Square]. Here he would meet with the regular visitors of the salon, representatives of the Jewish culture in Prague, such as writers Franz Werfel, Franz Kafka, Max Brod, indologist Moritz Winternitz, and Hugo Bergmann, librarian at the Klementinum Library. They would discuss philosophy and literature, Franz Kafka would sometimes read from his works, and there was music, too. Max Brod would play the piano and Albert Einstein the violin, his favorite instrument.

Einstein and his family left Prague after the end of the summer semester in 1912. He accepted another offer from the University of Technology in Zurich. It is possible that he conceded to his wife wishes to find a healthier climate for the children. He departed, all the while moving towards immortality and eternal recognition in theoretical physics and the Nobel Prize, which he received in 1921 for his discovery of the law of photoelectric effect. But his family life fell apart. The marriage of Mileva and Albert Einstein ended in divorce in 1919 on the grounds of "natural incompatibility". The year prior, Einstein wrote a letter to his wife in which he said: "I wonder what's going to last longer - the war or our marriage." Let us add, in defense of Einstein, that he gave the entire monetary amount he received in connection with the Nobel Prize to his former wife Mileva.

Einstein's older son, Hans Albert, became an engineer and professor of hydraulics at Berkley University, and chose to live his own life. The younger son, due to his strong psychic indisposition remained bound to his mother for the rest of her life. She was totally and selflessly devoted to him until her death on August 4, 1947, sacrificing virtually everything to him. Albert Einstein remarried soon after his divorce - to a close relative, his niece Elsa - whom he also survived. He himself died on April 18, 1955. In addition to the above mentioned plaques, there is a street bearing Einstein's name in Petrovice, Prague 10, where all the streets are named systematically after famous scientists.

In 1995, the media circulated an interesting piece of news, claiming that Einstein's son from his second marriage to Elsa probably lives in Prague. The rumor was spread by a certain machine engineer, Luděk Zakl, then 63, about himself. According to him, Elsa Einstein gave birth to him in 1932 at the Land Hospital *U Apolináře*. Fearing for the child's life, for reasons of his race, the boy was given to a certain Božena Zakl, who had just lost her own child due to a gross negligence of the maternity hospital workers. The major part of the archives of that hospital has been destroyed and it is unlikely that anyone would be able to find out the truth anymore. The sole important fact in the matter is that Ing. Luděk Zakl looks very much like the ingenious scientist.

Karel Škréta: The Siege of Prague by the Swedes in 1648.
Engraving by M. Merian Jr., Appendix to G. Schleder's
Theatrum Europaeum VI, (Frankfurt am Main 1663, (Prague -
National Museum)

Matthias Wenceslaus

JÄCKEL

One of the many artists who had come from near and far to enrich the appearance of Prague with his works of art was a Lusatian sculptor and carver, Matthias Wenceslaus Jäckel (1655 - 1738), or in the Sorbo-Lusatian language, his native tongue: Macij Wjaclaw Jakula. He holds a prominent position among the Bohemian Baroque sculptors, earning ever-increasing recognition with time. According to preserved documentation, the Lusatian sculptor arrived in Prague for the first time in 1684.

Matthias Wenceslaus Jäckel was born on September 11, 1655, in Kutov on the river Black Elstra in Upper Lusatia. His father was Johann Jäckel and his mother was Apolonia Jäckel. As young as fifteen, Jäckel went abroad to learn the ways of the world. During his travels he got as far as Italy where he stayed for an extended periods in Rome, Naples, and Venice. That is where he learned his trade. We have already said that he arrived in Prague in 1684. Within a very short time, on November 20, 1685, he got married. According to the records of St. Wenceslaus

Church on Malá Strana, he married Maria Elizabeth, the daughter of a deseased painter, Jan Hylbert. The couple's witness was another Malá Strana painter, Jan Bedřich Necker. After the wedding, the Jäckels lived in New Town Prague, where, on October 25, 1700, the artist purchased house No. 938, known as house *U Pinkavů* [Pinkava's House], for 730 guilders. New Town Prague accepted Jäckel on May 17, 1691, as a burgher, along with both of his sons, after he presented his marriage certificate and a proof of his Catholic background. He was doing very well, had no shortage of work, and his workshop was busy with two journeymen and both his sons working with him.

Jäckel created three series of sculptures for Karlův most [Charles Bridge], i.e., essentially the gallery of his art works. First, in 1707, there was a group sculpture with St. Anna in it, made of Žehrovice sandstone. This scultural group, considered the most lyrical, was made at the commission of Count Rudolf of Lisov, the master of Nový Stránov and Vtelna, district councilman and administrator of Old Town Prague. The lower part of the pedestal bears the emblem of the paying patron and on the side, there is the emblem of the patron's wife. The central figure of the sculpture is St. Anna who lived with her husband Joachim in Galilee in the city of Nazareth. At a relatively advanced age, a daughter was born to them, whom they called Miriam (God's beloved) - Mary. At the age of three, they took her to Jerusalem and deposited her at a convent to get education. St. Joachim died soon thereafter. The series shows Anna as a mature woman in a loose, long-girdled dress with veiled head. St. Anna is holding Jesus on her left arm and, with her right arm, embraces her daughter the Virgin Mary, who is looking up at her with an expression of devout respect in her face and giving her a bouquet of flowers. Little Jesus is holding a globe with a cross in his left hand and, with an expression of absolute confidence so characteristic for a child, is turned towards his grandmother.

In 1708, Jäckel created another sculptural group for the bridge gallery, with St. Thomas Akvinský and St. Dominik. Dating it is easy enough as it appears in the Latin text on the sash below the figure of the Madonna. In translation it reads: "For adornment of Jesus and Mary 1708." The commission to create this sculpture group came to Jäckel from the Dominican convent at the St. Aegidius Church in Old Town Prague. The central figure of the composition is Virgin Mary, holding Baby Jesus in her arms, in the company of the most prominent members of the Dominican order. One of them, St. Dominic, is kneeling in devoted worship as the Virgin Mary hands him a rosary. The scene is based on a legend in which the Virgin Mary appeared before St. Dominic near Toulouse and asked him to spread rosary payers among apostates as a means of drawing them back to faith. St. Dominic, the founder of the order of Dominican preachers, was sanctified by Pope Gregory IX, barely two years after his death. The third figure in the group is St. Thomas Akvinský, who is positioned symmetrically to St. Dominic. Second to the founder of the Order, this saint is considered the most important. He was exceptionally well-educated and is considered to have been the greatest scholar in the history of the Christian Middle Ages. He wrote several significant philosophical works.

The third and final of Jäckel's creations for Karlův most is a sculpture series made of sandstone with St. Bernard at its center. The artist sculpted this series in 1709 at the commission of Benedict Littwerig, the Abbot of the Cistercian Monastery in Osek. This fact is also indicated in an inscription which appears on a cartouche on the right side of the pedestal. The abundantly profiled scuptural group consists of three segments, with the middle raised to indicate the presence of clouds, with the heads of little winged angels peaking out from the clouds. The dominant figure is the Virgin Mary, holding Baby Jesus in her arms and a scepter in her right hand. Baby Jesus holds a globe in his left hand. A kneeling St. Bernard, the second founder of the Cistercian Order, is looking up in devotion at the Holy Mother and his position symbolizes that this saint, who is credited with bringing the greatest fame to the Cistercians, had entrusted the Order to her patronage. Jäckel dressed St. Bernard in a monastic robe and included an angel holding the symbol of the highest position in the order, the abbot's miter, before him. This clerical teacher is known to have repeatedly and intensively relived Jesus Christ's suffering on the cross. This is reflected in the left part of the sculpture. Apart from the indispensable angels, there also are the tributes of Jesus' torture and death: the cross, nails, hammer, and tongs. All this is complemented by the figures of a rooster and a veraicon, rendered in stone, as a reminder of a legend according to which a girl named Veronica, ignoring an enraged crowd, gave her hankerchief to the tortured and exhausted Jesus on his last route so he could wipe blood off his face. She was rewarded with a permanent impression of his face - the veraicon - on her hankerchief.

Of the other significant works of Jäckel in Prague, let us at least mention the statues standing on the portal of the former convent of the Paulan Order in northern section of Staroměstské náměstí, St. Thecla's altar in St. Joseph's Church in Malá Strana, the statues of the Apostles in the interior of the Jesuit St. Ignatius Church in New Town Prague, sculptures for the St. Francis Church of the Knights of the Cross in Old Town Prague, and many others. Last, but not the least, let us mention the sandstone sculpture series of St. Joseph with Jesus and four little angels of 1698, forming a part of the fountain on Karlovo náměstí in front of the New Town City Hall.

Quite unique is Jäckel's statue of St. Peter from 1728. It used to stand at first-floor level on the corner of the former Lužického Seminary, No. 90, on Malá Strana, in the direction of Míšeňská Street. The statue has all the attributes of the saint: a book and the keys to the heavenly kingdom. In 1987, the head of the statue loosened itself, fell to the ground and broke into thousands of pieces. Since there was no cast of the original available, a copy had to be reconstructed from historic photographs. A replica of the statue replaced the original in 1990. Jäckel's original statue of St. Peter was put in the depository. It is noteworthy that the building of the Lužického Seminary, which is believed to have been designed by Killian Ignatius Dientzenhofer, served in its time as an educational institution for those who came to Prague from Upper Lusatia to study. Thus Matthias Wenceslaus Jäckel had actually created the statue of St. Peter for his own countrymen.

The Lusatian sculptor and carver also created many pieces for the Bohemian countryside. For instance, the main altar for the St. Adalbert Church in Broumov, the statues of saints in Chotěšov, a double altar for the St. John Nepomuk and St. Vitus Cathedral consecrated to St. John Nepomuk in Dobřany near Stříbro, a sculptural group of St. Anna with the Virgin Mary on a bridge in Vyšší Brod, and a stone Madonna in the Cistercian Convent in Sedlec near Kutná Hora. The space in front of the church features a statue of St. Jan Nepomuk. The monastery in

Sedlec had given several commissions to Jäckel, probably partly due to the fact that his son Joseph was a monk there, under the monastic name Martin.

On August 25, 1724, Jäckel organized a wedding for his daughter Katarina. The groom was a sculptor named František Ignatius Weiss (+1756), whom Jäckel had sponsored so he could get a license to work in the city. The best man of the young couple was one of the most prominent Baroque sculptors, Ferdinand Maxmilian Brokof. After that Matthias Wenceslaus Jäckel, who had been employed in his craft for nearly 50 years, suffered some years of hardship. On December 13, 1733, he had his wife Maria Elizabeth buried,who, sources say, "... died at 66 of old age, after taking the last rites of the dying." As for Jäckel, who could no longer cope with the demands of sculpting and carving, it is said that he fell into poverty and accumulated many debts. After his wife died, he sold his house No. 938, *U Pinkasů*, in Jindřišská Street, including his workshop and equipment, to his son-in-law František Ignatius Weiss and his daughter for 1,000 guilders. Since the estate had been in debt in the amount of 933 guilders, he got less than 70 guilders upon signing the sale agreement.

The sculptor and carver Matthias Wenceslaus Jäckel died of old age in January 1738. The exact date of his death is unknown.

Jan Josef Dietzler: Third Courtyard with St. Vitus Cathedral, 1733. Watercolor-pen-ink drawing (Archives of the Prague castle)

Edward

KELLEY

An important era in the rich history of Prague is known under a specific, unmistakable name, a term of its own right: Rudolfinian Prague. The art-loving ruler, Emperor Rudolf II (1552 - 1612), who had made Prague his home base, would invite many prominent artists and scientists, for temporary or permanent assignments. Although the Emperor himself was an extraordinarily educated man, the age he lived in was an era booming with superstition. While mathematics, astronomy, and trigonometry were being developed to an unprecedented extent, so was also faith in astrology, i.e., teachings of direct links between planetary occurrences and the destiny of human beings. Simultaneously with the beginnings of genuine research in chemistry, the era also provided fertile soil for a pseudo-science called alchemy. The Emperor was not deaf to rumors claiming that gold could be manufactured artificially and so his court alchemists John Dee, Edward Kelley, Marco Bragadino, and many others enjoyed a rather cushy existence.

The most exemplary among them was Edward Kelley (1555 -1597), born Edward Talbot alias „Egelender", whose life and activities at the Court of Rudolf II had become legendary. Even *Ottův slovník naučný* [Otto's Encyclopedic Dictionary] mentions Kelley. He is believed to have been born in Worcester, England, and was a pharmacist by trade. Even in his native country, he used to profit from various swindles, fir which he was sentenced to have both ears cut off in a public execution place, as the customs of the time demanded. This was the reason why Kelley, the quack, wore long hair hanging down over his missing auricles. He had reportedly been given a much harsher sentence, a verdict of capital punishment, but it was eventually reduced to the above mentioned degrading sentence in return for the promise that he would conduct spying activities in Europe on behalf of the English Queen, Elizabeth.

Kelley's coming to Bohemia is attributed to his professional colleague, countryman, alchemist, and English scientist John Dee (1526 - 1608), who was working in Třeboň at the estate of Vilém z Rožmberka, a prominent Bohemian aristocrat, where he was commissioned to make gold. In his case, too, his alchemic activities were somehow concurrent with spying activities for the English Queen. For that reason he would often accompany his employer to Prague, to the Imperial Court, where he could always learn many of the interesting going-ons. He even got a short-term assignment as an alchemist with the Imperial Court.

In 1588, the two English alchemists ran into a very sharp conflict and parted ways. John Dee left Třeboň about a year later and, crossing Nuremberg, he returned to his homeland. But Kelley headed for Prague with the intention to serve the Emperor. He expected even greater financial and material support than he had been getting from the Rožmberks. He was not disappointed in his expectations.

But once in Prague, Kelley had to pass a proficiency examination. The first test he passed under a stern vigilance of the Emperor's counselor in natural sciences, Tadeáš Hájek z Hájku (1525 - 1600). The experiment was a „real success" as real gold appeared on the bottom of the beaker in which various chemicals had been heated. Tadeáš Hájek z Hájku immediately informed the Emperor who personally attended the second experiment, hoping that Kelley would help him fill his chronically empty imperial treasury. The second experiment was even "more successful". What's more, apart from gold, there also appeared a ruby. Kelley apologized saying that the tincture he used was too strong. Just how Kelley managed to fool both intelligent and highly educated gentlemen, for their time, and convince them of his skills remains a secret forever. We will never know whether Kelley used a double-bottomed beaker, or whether the mixing stick was hollows, or - an this is most likely the case - whether performed a skillful juggling trick.

The fact is that Edward Kelley had been the Emperor's favorite ever since. Given the position of a prominent court member, he had a constant access to the Emperor. For that reason, those who had no privileges like that and were in need of a favor from the Emperor, would buy themselves into Kelley's favors with smaller or larger bribes. Thanks to this circumstance, Kelley was able to acquire great wealth and buy several estates all over Bohemia. One of his properties was a sizeable house in New Town Prague, No. 502 and 503 at Dobytčí trh [Cattle Market] now Karlovo náměstí [Charles Square]. The large building closes off the southern side of the largest square in Prague and is commonly known as *Faust's house.* In 1590 Kelley reached the peak of his career in Rudolfinian Prague - he was knighted by Emperor Rudolf II.

Sometimes it happens that the higher one climbs, the harder one falls. Such was also Kelley's case. Just a year after he was knighted, he killed in a duel - an activity forbidden in Rudolfinian Prague - George Hunter, another of the Emperor's favorites. Anticipating that the Emperor's reaction would he harsh, he fled Prague, trying to get to southern Bohemia, to the estate of the Rožmberks, where he hoped to find asylum. However, he was trapped on the way down to the South, reportedly near Soběslav, and imprisoned - at the Emperor's explicit instructions in the *Huderka* [Huder's Tower] on Křivoklát Castle. The main reason for the Emperor's wrath was not only the above mentioned duel with fatal consequences, but also the fact that the Emperor had lost faith in Kelley's ability to make the much desired gold. The fact is that instead of filling the Emperor's treasury box, Kelley had succeeded during all the time spent in Prague only in making it emptier and emptier.

Despite that, Emperor Rudolf II did not give up on the belief that Kelley knew how to make gold. This assumption is confirmed by the fact that he, the Emperor, had Kelley tortured in the prison to extort from him the recipe for gold making. During that time, there were many delinquents imprisoned at the Křivoklát Castle and executions were nothing extraordinary. For that reason, the castle's captain always had an executioner handy to do the work. Since the current executioner at Křivoklát had just died and his successor had not as yet been assigned, Kelley, the alchemist, was interrogated by an executioner from Prague, a certain Jan Mydlář, the founder of a well-known executioners dynasty. Kelley was interrogated in the castle's torture room in the presence of imperial commissaries and a blood scribe. The manner of torture and interrogation of those days are known well enough so we can safely assume that Kelley would have eagerly disclosed any secret he could, but there was no secret recipe to tell.

The Empress herself intervened for Kelley's freedom with the Emperor - and let us add - to no avail, as well as Kelley's wife, Elizabeth Johanna Weston, an English woman, whom the alchemist married in Bohemia, where she had been living in religious and political exile. By marrying her, he became father to her two children, František and Alžběta, who later became a prominent Renaissance poetess, Elizabeth Johanna Weston (1582 - 1612). Among the intercessors on behalf of the Křivoklát prisoner was also the English Queen Elizabeth, who wrote a personal letter to Emperor Rudolf II, and the alchemist's former employer and supporter, Vilém z Rožmberka, a South-Bohemian aristocrat.

Kelley tried to escape from his tough prison. On a makeshift rope, he suspended himself at night from the window, after breaking through the iron bars. But the rope ripped and Kelley suffered a multiple, shattered fracture in his leg. Due to his injury, he was easily recaptured. His subsequent fate has been shrouded in many different legends. According to one of them, his leg healed partially, according to another, it was amputated and replaced with a wooden prosthesis. The fact is that Emperor Rudolf II did take mercy on him, after all, and released him. Heavily limping and penniless, for all his property had been confiscated by an order from the highest places, the alchemist went back to his lifestyle of swindle and ended up in prison, once again, on Castle Hněvín near Most. Here, according to a romanticized version, he made another unsuccessful attempt at escaping, breaking his good leg in three places. According to a more realistic version, he - in view of his hopeless situation - committed suicide in prison, by poisoning, sometime around 1597. He may well have used one of his quackish tinctures to release himself from his earthly ordeal.

Ludwig Kohl: Old Town Municipal Hall 1808; watercolor-pen-ink
drawing, (Prague - L. Sachs)

Johannes

KEPLER

O ne of the founders of modern astronomy, German physicist and mathematician, Johannes Kepler (1571 - 1630), arrived in Prague either at the end of December 1599 or the beginning of January 1600 from Graz where he was in the services of the an Austrian archduke. It was an era of religious discontent and Europe was experiencing ever-escalating disputes between the Catholics and Protestants. Precisely for that reason, Kepler felt no longer safe in Graz and gratefully accepted an invitation from his older and then more famous colleague, Tycho Brahe, to come to Prague. Tycho Brahe was conducting research as an astronomer at the court of Emperor Rudolf II and, before inviting Kepler, was obliged to ask permission from the Emperor. The Emperor agreed that Kepler might work with Tycho Brahe for a year or two. Their collaboration started at the castle in Benátky nad Jizerou, where Tycho Brahe had a second observatory, in addition to his Prague observatory.

Johannes Kepler was born on December 27, 1571, in a town

called Weil in Germany. Although he was the first child, he was probably born immaturely and therefore was weak and sickly. His father was Heinrich Kepler and his mother was Katarina, born Guldenmann. The role of family caretaker weighed especially heavily on the mother, as the father was an adventurer by nature and had himself recruited as a mercenary. Probably every famous personality is subject to legends about the reason for his taking this or another direction in life. For Kepler it was supposedly the year 1577, when he was less than six years old and his mother showed him a big comet in the sky. The legend continues to suggest that - citing an occasion when his father showed the boy a lunar eclipse three years later - the young boy's fixation on the stars had thereby been determined ever since. It is certain, though, that young Kepler's future then was still in the stars, literally. At thirteen, he enrolled in a monastery school, aiming to study theology and become a Protestant preacher. He was a brilliant student, excelling in every subject - Latin, especially. He was also very interested in mathematics, which however was not taught to any depth at the seminary. In his late teens, in 1589, he was admitted to the University of Tübingen, where he successfully passed - approximately two years thereafter - master degree examinations.

A decisive moment which changed Kepler's academic and scientific orientation was his meeting with Michael Mästlin, a professor of math and astronomy. He introduced him to the teachings of a Polish astronomer, a native of Toruň, Mikuláš Koperník (1473 - 1543), whose eager disciple he became. The decision was made. Kepler - fortunately for science - left his theological studies and, in 1594, accepted a vacancy for a teacher at an Evangelical school in Graz. He taught mathematics, rhetoric, and Latin literature. To stretch his salary a little, he would compile calendars for the next year, a common activity for his specialization in those days, and accept horoscope requests. He could never completely abandon horoscopes, not even as a world-famous astronomer much later on. In fact, he used to say: "What would dignified Mrs. Astronomy live off, if her light-footed daughter, Astrology, weren't making money in the streets?" He devoted his most intensive attention to his work on a book titled *Mystericum cosmographicum*. During that period, however, he found time enough to marry, and did so on April 27, 1597. His wife, Barbara

Müller, was a rich miller's daughter. Although only 23 years old, she was already twice a widow.

In Prague, Kepler lived first in Kurz's house on Pohořelec, upon the invitation of Tycho Brahe, who died very soon thereafter, in 1601. As Kepler stood at his death bed, his older colleague admonished him most suggestively to finish the Rudolfinian tables, i.e., new tables of the planets. Kepler, who had in the meantime fetched his family from Graz, moved to a now non-existing house on Dobytčí trh [Cattle Market], today's Karlovo náměstí [Charles Square] in New Town Prague. Emperor Rudolf II appointed Kepler Court Mathematician, with a salary of 1,000 guilders per year, and Tycho Brahe's successor.

Three children were born to the Keplers in Prague: Zuzana (* 1602), Friedrich (* 1604), and Ludwig (* 1607). At one point they moved, accepting gratefully the offer from one of Kepler's great friends and admirers, Rector of Charles University, Martin Bacháček of Neuměřice. From the Fall 1604, the family lived at the residential King Wenceslaus' College at Ovocný trh [Fruit Market] in Old Town Prague; house No. 537. It was there and then that Kepler reached the highest recognition for his discovery, namely, the fact that the planetary orbit is a perfect ellipse, with the planet Sun forming one of its foci. It was also at the King Wenceslaus College that Kepler completed the manuscript of his masterpiece titled *Astronomia Nova* [New Astronomy], in which he publicly explained the first two laws of planetary orbits. The first law states that each planet orbits around the Sun in an elliptic orbit, whereby the Sun is one of the foci of these elliptic orbits. The second law states that the line connecting the center of a planet and the center of the Sun always covers the same area over a certain time interval. This means that planets in the vicinity of the Sun orbit faster than the more distant ones.

Another Kepler's work, which guaranteed him a permanent place in the history of scientists-discoverers, was his *Dioptricum*, a work on the distribution of rays through an optical lens. This manuscript puts Kepler among the theoretical inventors of the astronomical telescope. It was characteristic for Rudolfinian Prague - and the era in general, in fact - that even a scientist of that format, such as Kepler certainly was, would be obliged to compose horoscopes. We would do so for the Emperor, for such was his duty, but also for the members of prominent Bohemian aristocratic families.

The last address of the Keplers in Prague was in Karlova Street in Old Town Prague, in house No. 188, called *U Francouzské koruny* [French Crown House] which has a passage to Anenská Street. From the courtyard of the house, one can see the tower in which Kepler had his observatory, in a house that belonged to a merchant named Udart. In 1971, on the occasion of the 400th anniversary of Kepler's birth, a commemorative plaque was unveiled on that house.

During those years in Prague, Kepler was in his prime. He would observe the skies with a borrowed telescope construed after Galileo Galilei's telescope; the two men maintained contact in writing. Kepler confirmed Galilei's discovery of Jupiter's moons and as of October 4, 1610, he had his own telescope which he construed with the assistance of Johann Matthias Wacker of Wackenfels. But fate was beginning to show its dark side. His wife Barbara fell seriously ill and all three children contracted small-pox, a very dangerous disease in those days. His six-year-old succumbed to the disease on February 19, 1611. Even the political situation was not very good. Disputes between the two Imperial brothers, Rudolf II and Matthias, came to a head. On February 15, 1611, the soldiers of the Passau Bishop Leopold Hapsburg besieged and looted Malá Strana. The Passauers, who had wanted to help strengthen the Emperor's shaken position, occupied Malá Strana until March 10, of the same year, but failed to conquer Old Town or New Town Prague. Consequently, Rudolf II had to give up his Bohemian crown in favor of his brother Matthias. Rudolf II stayed at the Prague Castle until his death on January 20, 1612.

Even before the death of his employer, Kepler, seeing the instability of the situation, left Prague and went to Linz, with his very ill wife. Shortly thereafter, merciless fate gave him another blow: on July 3, 1611, his wife died. What's more, the new man on the Bohemian throne, Matthias, would not hear of his predecessor's financial obligations to Kepler.

Another problem did not wait long to occur: Kepler's old mother was, along with a group of other people, accused of witchcraft in Württemberg, on account of her herbalist pursuits. This meant imprisonment, torture, trial, and death by burning at the stake. Such were the times. For instance, the year Kepler arrived in Prague, the astronomer Giordano Bruno was burned at the stake in Rome. After a formidable and nearly superhuman struggle, Kepler managed to save his mother from certain death. She walked out of the prison in a miserable state, weakened health, and died only a few months later.

Kepler went to Prague once more, towards the end of 1627, to deliver to the Emperor - another one in the succession, Ferdinand II - the promised Rudolfinian tables. The Emperor thanked him and rewarded him with a genuinely kingly generosity: he paid him 4,000 guilders. But continuation of research or pedagogical activities for Kepler in Prague were out of the question. Education was in the hands of the Jesuits and Kepler categorically refused to convert to Catholicism. He remained true to his faith, saying on the subject: "There are only two laws that I recognize: the law of the stars above me and the law of morality within me!"

The great astronomer had also worked for Albrecht von Wallenstein, for whom he composed the legendary horoscope which the famous warrior and builder of the Valdštejnský palác [Wallenstein Palace] on Malá Strana followed to a tee. At the invitation of Wallenstein, Kepler moved for a while to a Silasian town Zaháně and also stayed a few days on the estate of the Duke of Frýdlant in Jičín. Towards the end of his life, he settled in Linz where he was professor of mathematics. Johannes Kepler died on November 15, 1630, in Regensburg and is buried in the St. Peter's Cemetery there.

Since July 20, 1984, there stands a monument of two famous astronomers who had done work in Rudolfinian Prague: Tycho Brahe and Johannes Kepler. The monument is a joint creation of sculptor Josef Vajce and architect Vladimír Pýcha. Kepler's name can also be found on a red marble plaque on the front of the National Museum, below the second-floor window facing Čelakovský's Park. He was one of the many who had, like Čelakovský himself, done a lot for Czech science and culture. Needless to say, Tycho Brahe's name is among them.

Let us add a "plum": In *Národní Listy* of December 1, 1922, we have discovered an article which reviews a book of Václav Rosický titled *Staroměstský orloj* [Old Town Horologe]. The article mentions an inquiry, on record at the Municipal Archives, from the Committee for Kepler's Monument in Wrttemberg, asking whether it was the famous astronomer who had construed the Pražský orloj [Prague Horologe, also known as Old Town Horologe, see above].

F. K. Wolf: Deer Grove with Prague Castle, 1796; watercolor
engraving by A. Pucherna. Published by F. K. Wolf in 1803
(Prague - National Museum).

Oskar

KOKOSCHKA

T his world-renowned Austrian painter, known also as a successful writer and playwright, was born on March 1, 1886, in Pöchlarn, Northern Austria. But the Kokoschka family clan hailed from Bohemia. Both the grandfather and father Gustav had lived in Prague in a now demolished house called *U Ježíška* [Baby Jesus' House] in Spálená Street. They were goldsmiths by trade. Grandfather Václav, who hailed from Račiněves in the Podřipsko area, had once done restoration work on the St. Wenceslaus Chapel in the St. Vitus Cathedral at the Prague Castle. The Czech painter Quido Mánes used his likeness in a 1861 portrait titled 'Goldsmith'. Later, due to an unfavorable economic situation, the whole family moved to Austria.

After graduating from high school in 1904, Kokoschka was admitted to the School of Industrial Arts in Vienna, but was expelled after four years. The reason for this was the publication of his book, entitled *Die träumenden Knaben* [The Dreaming Boys] which he illustrated himself. In 1911 he returned to the same school in a completely different capacity - as an assistant professor.

Before WW I, Kokoschka painted primarily portraits. He freelanced for several magazines, and had his first one-man exhibition in Berlin. He became part of a new generation of artists. Among his friends was also Adolf Loss, an architect known to this day in Prague for his design of villa No. 642 in Střešovice for Dr. Ing. František Müller, a partner in a large construction company. Adolf Loss was quite instrumental in the sale of Kokoschka's first paintings; he commissioned a portrait of his wife, Bessie, from the painter, which was an incentive for others to follow suit.

Upon his return to Vienna, Kokoschka enraged the local petit-bourgeois in not just one, but two ways. Firstly, he maintained an openly amorous relationship with the young widow of the music composer Gustav Mahler, Alma Mahler; secondly, his exposition of paintings in Hagenbund was considered an outrage. During the time of his fling with Alma, he painted a well-known self-portrait with her. The exposition in Hagenbund was terminated before its scheduled closing date, after a personal intervention the successor to the throne, Archduke Ferdinand, who had also publicly made several pejorative statements about the painter. Kokoschka did not have it easy from the very start with those who were in power. The reason was that his work focused on the mission of man in this world, his ethical values, etc.

His prospective career was harshly interrupted by World War I. Obliged to join up, he nearly perished in the war. In 1915, he was most severely injured on the Halitch front. He suffered a bullet injury in the head and was injured with a bayonet in the chest; the bayonet had pierced his lungs. Nevertheless, he kept busy even during his long convalescence. While in the field hospital, only partly recovered, he wrote a play, *Orpheus and Eurydice*, whose motifs inspired Ernst Křenek, a music composer, to write an opera. As if to prove that no suffering or injury could stop him from working, he painted a portrait of his own mother in 1917.

After the end of W.W.I, Kokoschka accepted a position of a professor at the Dresden Academy of Fine Arts, where he stayed from 1919 until 1924. He traveled extensively thereafter, staying a long time in France, Holland, England, Turkey, and

Northern Africa. In 1931, he settled in Vienna. However, the onset of Nazism and change in the political climate forced him to make a radical decision.

At the end of the summer of 1934, Oskar Kokoschka came to Prague, seeking a quiet place of refuge after the Nazis launched a fierce campaign against him. He moved into fourth floor of Hotel *Juliš* on Václavské náměstí. He went back to his roots, so to speak, for both his grandfather and father used to live in Prague. Another reasons was that his sister, married to a Czech, was also living in Prague. Thanks to President T. G. Masaryk, Kokoschka was granted Czechoslovak citizenship in 1935, which proved very useful three years later, when he decided to emigrate to London.

During his stay in Prague, Kokoschka took the side of anti-Fascist intelligentsia. As president of the Liberal German Cultural Union he also advocated unification of emigrants, based on anti-Fascist principles. As a humanitarian and artist - who had personally experienced the horrors of war - he created a lithographic poster titled *Help Basque Children*. Hanging posters in public areas was strictly forbidden by law. The restriction was intended to prevent the development of a crisis in diplomatic relations between Prague and Berlin.

The Nazis organized a major exhibition of works of creative arts in Germany which they titled *Entartete Kunst* (Perverted Art), displaying Kokoschka's works, among others. The artist responded with a self-portrait that he titled, sarcastically of course, *Self-portrait of a Perverted Artist*. The Nazis had confiscated a total of 417 of Kokoschka's works from both public and private collections.

During his stay in Prague, Kokoschka led a very active social life, attending, for instance, all the performances of Voskovec and Werich at their *Liberated Theater*. His most frequent companion in Prague was Dr. Hugo Feigl, a, art gallery owner and brother of the painter Bedřich Feigl. Somewhere, somehow, in the whirl of social life, Kokoschka met his future wife, Olda Palkovská, daughter of a connoisseur and collector of fine arts, Dr. Břetislav Palkovský.

Up to this day, the pieces created by Kokoschka in the years 1934 - 1938 on Prague themes form a distinct and important group among his works. The artist painted a total of eight views of Prague: from the terrace of *Kramářova villa*, a famous view of the Charles Bridge, a view from Smetanovo nábřeží [Smetana's water front], from a window of the Strahov Monastery, from Schönborn Palace, from Kampa, and from a window of the Monastery of the Knights of the Cross. One of these paintings, the legendary Panorama of Prague was on display in 1994 in the then newly opened commercial gallery, the prestigious *Peter Brandl Art Gallery* in Prague. The price was 19 million CZK. The National Gallery immediately put it aside to ensure that so significant a piece of art would remain in the Czech Republic.

Oskar Kokoschka's studio was in a prime Prague location, in a corner house, No. 329, called *Bellevue*, on today's Smetanovo nábřeží, then called Masarykovo. From the window of his studio Kokoschka could look over the whole magnificent historic panorama of Prague, the Vltava river, Kampa, Petřín, Charles bridge, Malá Strana, the Prague Castle, and Hradčany. With respect to Masarykovo being the former name of the water front, let us mention that T.G. Masaryk and Oskar Kokoschka were friends and had great respect for each other. In fact, Kokoschka painted a portrait of the Czechoslovak President Masaryk. It was sold to the United States of America and the proceeds were donated for humanitarian purposes.

The year 1938 brought along the Munich Treaty, which altered the fate of Czechoslovakia, and Kokoschka, for whom staying in Prague represented dreadful danger, had to flee to London with his wife-to-be to London. His idle studio on Smetanovo nábřeží was later taken over by Jiří Trnka. Perhaps to show that leaving Prague had not been an easy decision for him, Kokoschka painted a very large panorama of Prague, during his stay in the city above the river Thames, which he called Prague Nostalgia. This is the eighth painting which was missing in the above account of his paintings of Prague.

Upon their arrival in London, Kokoschka and Olda Palkovská married and continued to live there for 15 years. As before, he traveled extensively, visiting Ireland, Scotland, Switzerland, Italy, and even America. Kokoschka never returned to Czechoslovakia which had meanwhile undergone its "Victorious February" [a Communist putsch].

During the summer months of the years 1953 - 1962, he taught painting in Salzburg, at the School of Images which he himself founded. Over the period of the school's existence, there also were some students from Bohemia. This activity enabled Kokoschka to relive his teaching career at the Viennese School of Industrial Arts. As in the past, he also continued to write and even compose music. The painted, graphic artist, writer, and playwright Oskar Kokoschka died at a very old age of almost 94 years, on February 21, 1980, in Switzerland.

In conclusion, let us recall the 1986 exhibition of his works at Anežský Convent, Prague, and the 1991 exhibition of a rare collection of his graphics at Kinský Palace in Old Town Prague. The latter exhibition was possible only thanks to the generous gift from Kokoschka's wife Olda who gave the National Gallery a collection of 95 graphics which the artist created over a period of twenty years, from 1950 to 1970. Mrs. Olda Kokoschka visited Prague in November 1991 to attend the Czech premiere of her husband's drama play, *Comenius*, which he had written during his stay in Prague. Staged by T. Juřička and J. Someš, the premiere took place at *Divadlo na Starém Městě* [Old Town Theater], formerly *Divadlo Jiřího Wolkra* [Jiří Wolker's Theater].

Antonín Mánes: View of Hradčany from the East, about 1820; oil
(Prague - National Museum)

Franz

*L*ISZT

O ne of the number of excellent world-famous music
composers and interpreters who were no strangers to
the city of 100 spires on the Vltava river, Prague, was
the Hungarian composer and piano virtuoso, Franz Liszt (1811 -
1886). Liszt visited Prague on several occasions. Especially his
first arrival in 1840 was expected with enormous interest and
enthusiasm. The whole Europe applauded Liszt at that point,
according to detailed articles in contemporary Prague
newspapers and magazines, but music-loving Pragonians had
not, until that year, had the chance to hear the
Maestro's concert in Bohemia.

Franz Liszt was born on October 21, 1811, in Doborján, to
Adam and Anna Liszt. His father, of noble descent, played the
violin, piano, and guitar. His mother, born Lager, hailed from
Kremms in Lower Austria. She was partly German. During the
year in which Franz Liszt was born, a large comet was passing
over the sky. This was taken by the family as a good sign for
the newborn. But at first, the opposite seemed to be the case -

the child was weak and sickly. At one point, when little Franz was three years old and lying deeply unconscious for days, the situation looked so hopeless that a joiner was called to take measurements for a coffin. But the child survived and, in fact, the older Franz grew, the stronger he became.

Soon enough, it became apparent that the child has an extraordinary talent for music when he would hum whole music passages played by his father on the piano. When asked what he wants to become when he grows up, he said: a musician. According to a legend, he would point at a painting on the wall, saying he wanted to be "like that man up there..." - long before he was old enough to know who Beethoven was. The painting was a portrait of Beethoven. His first music teacher was his father. Recognized as a child prodigy, Franz Liszt began to give concerts at a very young age. Another legend claims that when his hands were too little to play the octaves in more demanding music compositions, he would help himself with his nose.

For reasons of the boy's great talent, the family moved to Vienna, where his father could make arrangements for proper musical education. One of his piano teachers was even Carl Czerny (Karel Černý), whose parents had also moved to Vienna, from Nymburk, to pursue their son's gift for music. Franz Liszt gave his first concert in Vienna in 1822. During one of his subsequent concerts, young Liszt met Ludwig van Beethoven. Beethoven was enthusiastic over his playing, although we know that he was practically deaf then - another legend challenged... It is said that Beethoven picked Liszt up, kissed him on the forehead and predicted a great future for him.

The prophesy began to come true. He traveled everywhere with his father, due to his young age, and played all over Europe, delighting audiences with his playing and perfect musical ear. Vienna, Budapest, Paris, and London - these were the main venues of his triumphs. Apart from public concerts, he would also give private concerts, primarily in aristocrats' palaces. At that time, he also began to compose music. Just as he reached the first peak of fame and recognition, he encountered the dark side of life. On August 28, 1827, his father died, after a short spell of sickness.

Liszt continued on his way up in his starry career, earning

a great success also in Italy. He also found time enough to fall in love. Actually, he attracted women throughout all his life. His female admirers would kiss his hands, carry his likeness in their broaches, keep the coffee grounds or tea leaves from his cups in tiny bottles, wear the butts of his cigars on their necklaces, and one American woman even got hold of the fabric from the chair in which had been sitting.

And now, Franz Liszt was to come to Prague! The whole city, Bohemian and German quarters alike, was excited over his arrival. The echoes of the most recent cultural event - the first Bohemian public ball, held on February 5, 1840, at the Konvikt Hall - have barely died down when, in the same month, such a prominent person as Liszt was due to arrive. All the newspapers, such as *Europe, Bohemie, Úřední listy, Včela,* and *Květy* wrote about this unique composer of *Hungarie* and *Uherské rapsodie,* a piano virtuoso, a man of worldwide fame - Franz Liszt. Although the ball season was not over yet, Liszt certainly became the program of the season, without competition. His success and achievements were discussed in all the salons, cafés, theaters, and the promenades of Prague.

February went by and Liszt would still not come, although the preliminary schedule of his concerts had already been announced. On March 3, 1840, on Mardi Gras, a grand ball was taking place at Stavovské Theater in Old Town Prague. Hundreds of merry, colorfully-dressed dancing gentlemen and ladies were frolicking about the theater, the Baron Baillet-Latour's orchestra from the 28th regiment, conducted by Josef Liehmann, played music on a decorated balustrade in the middle of the stage. All this went on and on until midnight, when the bells in St. Havel's Church nearby struck the hour. When the bells stopped, the orchestra played the obligatory fanfare - a sign that the face masks must be removed. The ball guests started to undo their masks, as usual, but the fanfare did not stop. After a short moment of uncertainty about what was going on, the people broke out into a deafening euphoria and applause.

In a red-velvet covered loggia stood an artist with long hair, pale face, gracefully built. In his hand he held a black mask and next to him stood his admirer, hostess, and escort in Prague, Baroness Elisa Šlik. Liszt was finally in Prague.

The next day, Liszt visited the leading personality in the

music scene of Prague, composer Václav Jan Tomášek, at his home at 15 Tomášská Street, in a house called *U Klárů* [Klárs' House]. There is a bilingual commemorative plaque on that house today. Liszt was accompanied by a Prague merchant with sheet music, Jakub Fischer, who had exclusive rights to all the tickets for Liszt's concerts in Prague.

The first concert took place in the grand salon of house No. 416, named *Platýz* [Flounder], whose front facade today faces Národní třída. Although the ticket prices were relatively high - three, two, and one guilder - the auditorium was sold out. Liszt's co-performers were Kateřina Podhorská, member of the opera ensemble of Stavovské Theater, and Karel Strakatý, a well-known singer. At the end of the concert, Liszt gave in to the applauding audience and added several compositions. The last encore was his *Chromatic Gallop*. The success of the young piano genius in Prague was so enormous that he ended up giving six concerted, instead of the scheduled three. A noteworthy detail is that he donated the proceeds from one of the concerts to the hospital *U alžbětinek* at Na Slupi and the proceeds from another concert went to the Institute of the Blind.

In memoriam of the great Hungarian composer and pianist, a plaque was mounted on the facade of the *Platýz* house, to the right of the portal on the corner of Uhelný trh [Coal Market] and Martinská Street, on the mezzanine level. The inscription on the white marble plaque announces: "F. Liszt - in the years 1840 - 1846, this house resonated with his music." The plaque is complemented by a bust of Franz Liszt, a 1962 work of Hana Wichterl.

The first of Liszt's concerts in Prague was also attended by a sixteen-year-old admirer, Bedřich Smetana. Overwhelmed by the Maestro's brilliant technique and ability to communicate with the audience, Smetana confided, during his high school studies in Pilsen, in his diary: "...in composition I want to be a Mozart and in technique a Liszt." In 1848, when Smetana suffered a severe crisis, he resolved to turn to Liszt for help, aware of his legendary charity. In a letter describing all his problems, he asked him for financial help, promising to repay him as soon as his situation improves. In the letter he also enclosed his composition, Opus 1, asking Liszt to accept it and use his influence to help the composition find its way into concert halls. Liszt obliged and sent Smetana 450 guilders. Later on, the two composers, who had much respect for one another, met several more times and remained lifelong friends.

During a tea party at the salon of Baroness Šlik, who herself was an excellent pianist, the Prague circle of music fans attending the tea party were stunned when Liszt sat down to the piano and played a brilliant improvisation on the motifs of Bohemian folklore songs. His Bohemian friends were even more astonished over him profound interest in the Hussite tradition and especially Hussite songs. Unfortunately, there were none at hand in written form, not even the legendary Hussite hymn *Ktož jsú boží bojovníci* [Who are God's Warriors...]. Baroness Šlik then offered Liszt, as a substitute, another revolutionary song popular among Bohemian patriots at the beginning of the 19th century.

Franz Liszt visited Prague several times thereafter, but the exact number of his visits could not be traced. Sometimes he would come for health reasons, spending time in one of the spas in Northern or Western Bohemia. The last time he gave a piano concert in Prague was in 1846. He performed in the *Platýz* house, again; in the Konvikt Hall, at Konviktská Street No. 291 in Old Town Prague; and in another place famous for its music and ball tradition - the grand salon of the Žofín restaurant. In 1856, Liszt came to Prague once more to conduct the Prague premiere of the *Estergom Mass*. The dress rehearsal fell on Saturday, September 27, the premiere was to be the next day. Historic records state that there were 4,000 people in the Cathedral on that day. We must realize that this was before the Cathedral's completion, i.e., in a much smaller space created by Matthias of Arras and Peter Parler.

After spending some time as the court conductor in Weimar, where he also founded and managed a music school, Liszt did something that really surprised his friends and supporters - to put it mildly. On April 25, 1865, he had himself consecrated and donned a cassock. The last period of his life he devoted to church music. Apart from the *Estergom Mass*, let us recall the *Coronation Mass, Cantata for St. Cecile, Oratorio for Jesus,* and Oratorio *Legend of St. Elizabeth.* He did not finish his last composition, *Oratorio for St. Stanislav.* The Oratorio *Legend of St. Elizabeth* had its Prague premiere in 1866 at Novoměstské Theater in New Town Prague, conducted

by Bedřich Smetana. Smetana informed Liszt about it in
a letter dated May 15, 1866.

The phenomenal piano virtuoso and music composer, Franz
Liszt, died at midnight on July 31, 1886, in Bayreuth, Bavaria.
He was buried modestly, without any ceremony, on August 3, at
the local cemetery. Such was his wish in his last will. On
August 28, in the same year, the National Theater in Prague
organized a mourning ceremony in his honor.

Jan Josef Dietzler: Malá Strana, Hradčany, die Stone (Charles)
Bridge; pen-and-ink drawing, about 1730 (Vienna - Count von
Liechtenstein's collection of maps)

Lorenzo

Of Brindisi

O n Loretánské náměstí on Hradčany stands a simple
single-bay sacral structure, the Church of *Panny
Marie Andělské* [Angelic Virgin Mary's], which forms
part of the Capuchin Monastery. It is the largest structure of the
Capuchin Order in Bohemia, both from the perspective of the
structure's prominent location and the urban aspects of it. Four
hundred years have passed since its foundations were laid. At
that time, twelve members of the Capuchin Order, led by
Lorenzo of Brindisi (1559 - 1619), later sanctified, arrived in
Bohemia from Italy.

Born on August 22, 1559, he was originally called Julius
Caesar Rossi and hailed from Brindisi in southern Italy. He
adopted his monastic name, Lorenzo, in 1575, when he joined
the Capuchin noviciate in Verona, a new branch of the
Franciscan Order whose aim was to revive the ideals of Francis
of Assisi. Lorenzo had a phenomenal memory. It is said, for
instance, that he knew practically the whole Bible by heart. He
learned languages easily - he knew Hebrew, Greek, and several

others, including dialects. He studied at the University of Padova, Italy. He is known to have been an excellent speaker whose sermons were unequaled in their time. Gradually, he would attain ever higher positions in the Capuchin Order

At the turn of the 16th century, most of Europe - and Prague was no exception - was jolted about by religious, and therefore also political, unrest. Prague, the seat of Emperor Rudolf II, was divided between the Catholics and Protestants, becoming one of foci where the battle the two camps was fought. The Emperor, relying primarily on his clerks in state business, was unable to take sides. Though raised in an orthodox Catholic environment, he did not want to alienate the Bohemian gentry, whose many members were more in favor of the Protestant faction. Emperor Rudolf II was also irritated by the excessive zeal of the Pope's nuncios emitted to Prague. He resented Rome's Pharisaic ways. What's worse, the impending war with Turkey was a threat. It eventually broke out, on August 27, 1593, in Budapest and Constantinople, when Sultan Murad III made a formal declaration of war to Emperor Rudolf II, after many military skirmishes of various intensity.

The whole situation was also addressed by the Trident Catholic Convention; the decision was, inter alia, that the Capuchins should be sent any place where Protestantism made progress so that the Catholic faith might be defended. The recommendations of the Convention were eventually accepted even by Emperor Rudolf II. The Archbishop of Prague officiating at that time, Zbyněk Berka of Dubé, could then ask Pope Clement VIII to send Capuchins to Bohemia. So, on November 13, 1599, thirteen members of the Capuchin Order arrived in Prague, led by Lorenzo of Brindisi. Apart from him, there were six priests, three clergyman, and three layman. Their journey was incredibly hard, because, in accordance with the regulations of their Order, they made the whole trip on foot. At first, Zbyněk Berka of Dubé put them up in his house on Hradčany and then gave them shelter in the general headquarters of the Order of the Knights of the Cross at the bridgehead of Karlův most [Charles Bridge] in Old Town Prague - for he was not only an Archbishop, but also the headmaster of the Knights of the Cross and Red Star. That is where the Capuchins, especially Lorenzo of Brindisi, took up preaching on behalf of the Catholic faith. They learned Czech very fast and their sermons became very popular.

Both the Archbishop of Prague, Zbyněk Berka z Dubé, and Lorenzo of Brindisi could see that the provisory shelter would not last long. They went around together, looking for a suitable plot of land for the construction of a Capuchin monastery and church. The place they chose was quite far from downtown Prague then. It was in the lower section of today's Loretánské náměstí. Formerly, there was a garden which belonged to Markéta Lobkowitz. The Capuchins bought this land as a site for their structures with an existing house, owned by Jan Vopička, a mason, and his sister. In May 1600, the Capuchins brought a large wooden cross to the building site and the construction of the monastery and church could begin. The structures were built according to instructions of Lorenzo of Brindisi, "in a simple style", as the Order's regulations stipulated. The construction proceeded very quickly, with substantial support from Catholic gentry. The largest contribution was made by Archbishop Zbyněk Berka of Dubé. It was also he who consecrated the Church of the Angelic Virgin Mary in 1602. Imperial Regent Jan Fernemont donated to the new holy place a statue of the Virgin Mary which had been set aflame by the Calvinists in 1550; she had lain in the fire for 12 hours without any harm at all.

The Capuchin church became known also for the dispute between the brethren and the famous Danish astronomer Tycho Brahe (1546 - 1601), who was doing his research in Prague at that time. He had his observatory on the adjacent property and was terribly irritated by the constant ringing, even before the church was finished, of the bells in the Capuchin church. The dispute came to a head, but found no solution, as its very substance was the dispute between two antagonist camps, the Catholics and Protestants. It went so far that the Emperor Rudolf II himself had to step in, but the whole affair did not conclude until the death of the famous astronomer. Even before that, the Capuchins were all but expelled from Prague by the Emperor after their enemies convinced him that the Capuchins were plotting against his life. Older literary sources indicate that the rumor had been started by Tycho Brahe himself, who claimed to have read about the imminent murder of the king in the stars. The Emperor's butler, in turn, managed to fool the Emperor by telling him the citizens of Prague knew for fact that his occasional heartburn is caused by the prayers of the

Capuchins. The truth about all the intrigues against Lorenzo of Brindisi and, by extension, the Capuchin Order, and their true relations with the Emperor are concealed under 400 years of time elapsed since.

In 1602, Lorenzo of Brindisi was elected to General of the Capuchin Order in Rome. He would take many inspection trips, as was his duty, not only all over Italy, but also Germany, Switzerland, France, and Spain. This weakened his already fragile health and as early as 1605 he passed his high office to priest Sylvester of Assisi. Despite that, in 1607, he walked all the way to Prague again at the wish of Emperor Rudolf II who wanted him to take up the practice of giving mass to Pragonians again. Lorenzo of Brindisi stayed in Prague until 1609 and throughout that time he organized scholarly debates at the Capuchin monastery on the theme of true faith.

Lorenzo of Brindisi spent the last years of his life alternately at the Capuchin monastery in Venice, and journeys in Spain and Portugal. He died on July 22, 1619, in the capital city of Portugal, Lisbon. He was buried in Villafrance, on the grounds of a convent of Franciscan nuns (Clares). Pronounced blessed in 1783, Lorenzo of Brindisi was sanctified on December 8, 1881, by Pope Leo XIII. Pope John XXIII declared him a spiritual mentor, an honor which the Catholic church reserves for very few of their members.

Lorenzo's great accomplishment, the foundation and construction of the Capuchin monastery and Church of *Panny Marie Andělské* [the Angelic Virgin Mary] in Prague on Hradčany stands in on its spot to this day, resisting the wear of time through centuries, war events, and enemies of faith. After 1989, when the political situation changed, the Capuchin monks returned to take care of the dilapidated property. Their church and monastery are very popular both among Pragonians and visitors to the city, among other things for their unique Christmas crêche which dates back to 1780. The crêche has 43 life-size figures which an unknown member of the Capuchin order worked on for over 10 years. The bodies of the figures are modeled out of straw, supported by wooden skeletons. They are dressed in contemporary clothing and reinforced so firmly with glue that time could not destroy them. There are also fifteen sheep which used to have real sheepskin, however, those did not withstand time and had to be replaced with plaster which is finely worked into curls to resemble real fleece. The crêche can always be viewed at Christmas, but prospective viewers need to be prepared to stand in line for a while, because of the site's popularity.

Sam. Prout: St. Mikuláš [Nicholas] Church in Malá Strana,
Prague, about 1820; lithograph
(Prague - Klub Za Starou Prahu / Club for Old Prague)

MARIA ELECTA

Ever since the middle ages, Prague was the seat of
numerous clerical orders. Already around 970, the first
convent was founded under the St. George Church at
the Prague Castle. The position of the Abbess of the Benedictine
Convent was filled by Mlada, daughter of Boleslav I. The St.
George Church was subsequently rebuilt so as to suit the needs
of the new convent. The first monastery in Bohemia was built in
993 by bishop Vojtěch in Břevnov, at that time still considered
some distance from Prague. It was also a Benedictine
monastery and was inhabited by monks from Monte Cassino in
Italy. Other monasteries and convents followed; some of them
were founded and built even under King Charles IV as part of
his grand project: the development New Town Prague.

Let 's now skip three centuries, which gets us to the Thirty
Years' War, to the era of Emperor Ferdinand III (1608 - 1657),
who reigned from 1637 to 1657. He made a pledge with God,
promising him that if he might live to see the end of the war, he
would build St. Joseph's church and monastery in Prague for the

Order of Barefooted Carmelites. For that purpose he purchased, in 1655, house No. 43 on Malá Strana, for 26,000 guilders, from Ferdinand Count Wallenstein. He had the house, which had a large garden, remodeled into a temporary convent. The convent's first inhabitants were 17 sisters from Krakow, who had been expelled from their homeland during the war and this convent was to be their asylum. Five sisters of the same Order same from Vienna and Graz, for whom the convent was originally designated. One of them was so ill that she had to be carried in on a covered stretcher. The Mother Superior of these Carmelite sisters was a prominent member of the Order, Maria Electa. The second day upon arriving in Prague, she was appointed Vicaress of the new convent by the General of the Order, who was in Prague just then.

Maria Electa was born in an Italian town, Terni, and christened on January 7, 1605, as Katarina. Her parents were Alexius Tramazoli and his wife Eutropia. According to a legend about her birth, she was born with a very fine complexion so that it seemed that the little girl had a white dress on. For that reason, people predicted that she would become a nun and called her a "holy child". During her childhood and teenage years, she was truly different from her contemporaries. On June 2, 1626, Katarina Tramazoli, together with her sister Lucia, who was 4 years older, joined the Order of the Blessed Virgin Mary on Carmel. This Order was founded in the middle of the 12th century by a crusading knight, St. Berthold, in Mount Carmel Holy Land near the cave of Prophet Elias. In the 16th century, the Order was reformed by St. Therese of Aville and St. John of the Cross. Lucia Tramazoli got a monastic name, Jarolíma of the Holy Spirit, and Katarina Tramazoli was from them on called Electa of St. John, God's Beloved.

According to a legend, the Abbess of the Convent in Terni had a vision that Electa should no longer be of Electa St. John but Maria Electa of Jesus - and so she became. From the convent in her hometown, Maria Electa was transferred to Vienna, where she stayed for 14 years. When the deeply religious Emperor, a great supported of the Carmelites, Ferdinand II, founded another Carmelite convent in Graz, Maria Electa became the founding sister there. In 1654, the building of the convent and church were completed and, after a Holy Mass, the convent was closed and confinement procedures were carried out. Together with Maria, there were 16 other Carmelite sisters confined there.

Was we have said above, the Carmelite sisters came to Prague in 1656, led by Maria Electa, who was then called off to help found another convent. The sisters walked across Stará Boleslav and, after performing all the necessary spiritual procedures, including holy communion, they arrived to Prague on September 1, 1656, in the afternoon. Their first duty on Prague soil was to serve a mass in the Carmelite Church of Virgin Mary the Victorious, which is well-known in all the Christian world for its statue of *Baby Jesus of Prague*. The sisters were welcomed by the Archbishop of Prague, Count Arnošt Harrach, and a crowd of believers. After a ceremonial welcome, the Carmelites walked - led by Maria Electa - to their temporary convent.

All sources claim that Maria Electa was exceptionally religious, hard-working, and had many other virtues. The sisters feared she would be called off again to help found another Carmelite convent and they would lose their beloved Mother Superior. They therefore begged the General of the Order to promise them that she would stay in Prague for at least three years. On June 20, 1660, Maria Electa was elected to become Prioress of the Convent of the Barefooted Carmelites in Prague. Her main role was to organize the construction of the convent buildings. But she never saw the well-started work completed. She fell seriously ill and her conditions was getting progressively worse. Orthodox adherence to frequent fasting certainly did not help improve her condition. Plagued by frequent headaches, liver dysfunction, spitting of blood, the Prioress even became paralyzed in one leg. Reputed to be a saint, Maria Electa died in her convent cell on January 11, 1663. The oak coffin which had been made for the Prioress turned out to be too short, so her neck had to be broken...

She was buried in the convent's garden, in a shallow cellar in the middle of the St. Elias Chapel. The chapel was built in the 17th century as an artificial cave with frescoes on the ceiling. On a small altar, there stood a statue of St. Joseph made by Matthias Wenceslaus Jäckel. We can assume that this used to the Prioress' favorite place and that it was her wish to be buried there. A real burial in the convent or the church crypt was not possible, because neither of them was completed when Maria

Elekta died. The St. Elias Chapel is situated in the former convent garden, *Vojanovy sady* today, but it is in a dilapidated condition.

For reasons of an expected flood, Maria Electa's body was exhumed three years later and, to a great astonishment, it was found that - beneath the disintegrated clothing - her body was intact, despite the fact that the cellar was completely under water. The stunned sisters took the body of their Prioress, to the Convent, to let the body dry out. They washed her with boiled wine, rose petals, rosemary, and lavender. As a consequence of this well-meant procedure, Maria Electa's complexion turned brown. Assuming that vinegar compresses would bleach her skin, they were terrified to see that the opposite was true. Her face turned black. That is what her face is like to this day.

During the Baroque era, the integrity of her body was considered a miracle, of course. Her body was examined by reputed medical specialists, including the representatives of the Prague University, and reports were written stating that her body is intact, indeed. What's more, her body expelled a liquid which smelled like jasmine. A report was duly sent to the Pope and the Imperial Court in Vienna.

Maria Electa performed miracles not only during her life, but also after her death. It is said that the sick got well after touching her grave. But it is believed that the greatest miracle happened to her own body. The sisters thought it would be appropriate to seat the former Prioress on a chair, but this was not possible due to rigor mortis. The Mother Superior then ordered Maria Electa to be obedient, as she always had been during her life. And behold, rigor mortis disappeared and her body became quite pliable; so Maria Electa was dressed up in the usual Carmelite garments and seated on a chair. After displaying their Prioress at the newly completed St. Joseph Church, and completing the construction of the convent, the nuns took her body to a special chapel where she can be seen, sitting up, through a barred window. Many claim that her body emits a pleasant smell, or that Maria Electa opens her eyes and turns her eyes. There even were some who claimed to have spoken with the former Prioress.

In 1781, the nuns were asked to assume a duty in educating the youth of Prague, but due to strict regulations of their Order and confinement, they could not oblige. For that reason, the

Convent of the Barefooted Carmelites on *Malá Strana* in Prague was liquidated by the decision of Emperor Joseph II. At that time, there were 19 nuns in it, thereof 9 aristocratic women from very prominent families, such the Kounics, Kolovrats, and others. The sisters moved out to live in another - Cistercian - Convent, which had also been liquidated, in Pohled near German Brod, today Havlíčkův Brod. They took their former Prioress, Maria Electa, whom they honor as a saint, with them, in a light wooden cabinet. They chose their route so as that their former Prioress could always spend the night in a church. In Čáslav, impatient admirers of this saint pushed against the cabinet, eager to see the saint with their own eyes, and the cabinet was damaged. But the Carmelite sisters restituted her immediately to her former condition.

Forced exile of the Carmelites in Pohled ended after ten years, when Emperor Leopold II donated them a former Barnaby monastery on Hradčany Square in Prague. In the same year, the sisters moved back to the capital city of the Bohemian Kingdom and the first Prioress of the Prague Carmelite Convent, the honorable Maria Electa, returned to Prague with them. Her body is situated in the epistolary, i.e., to right side of the altar, in an enclosed cabinet, where thousands of visitors can see her thorough a barred window.

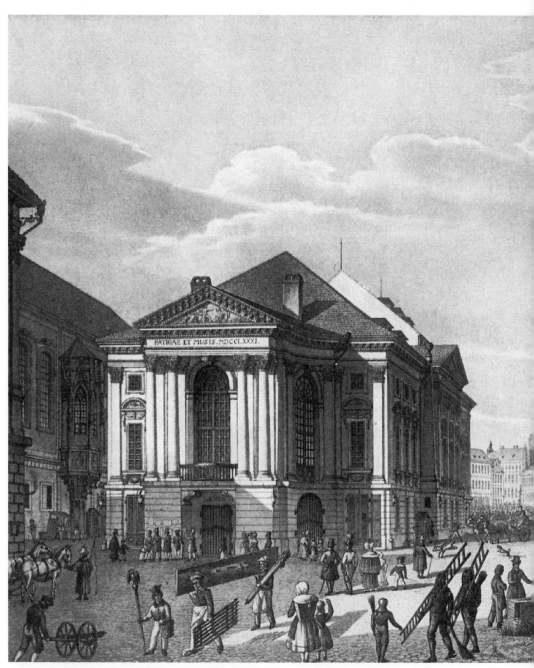

Vinzenc Morstadt: Prague, Stavovské Theater, about 1830, sepia
drawing (Prague - Municipal Museum)

Wolfgang Amadeus

MOZART

T he name of this ingenious music composer, Wolfgang Amadeus Mozart (1756 - 1791), who holds the foremost position in the history of music, is inseparable from Prague. After all, he had spent time here from 1787 until 1791 five times in all, sometimes for a short period, other times longer. His relationship to his Prague hosts, Mr. and Mrs. Dušek, was legendary, but especially famous was his relationship with a beautiful opera singer, Josephine Dušek, born Hampacher (1754 - 1824). No less legendary became his exclamation on the memorable evening, October 29, 1787. After the end of Mozart's opera *Don Giovanni*, which had its Prague and simultaneously world premiere at the Stavovské Theater in Old Town Prague, as it seemed that the applause of the audience would never stop, the great master of tones and melodies declared: "My Pragonians understand me." Ever since then, these words have been repeated over and over in favor of and to the honor of music loving Prague.

Wolfgang Amadeus Mozart was born on January 27, 1756, in

Salzburg. His parents, who got married in 1747, were Leopold
Mozart and Anna Maria, born Pertl. They had several children,
one after the other, reaching number seven, but only two of
them lived to see their first birthday. There was Maria Anna,
born July 30, 1751, and son Wolfgang Amadeus, a future music
genius. His talent for music he probably inherited from his
father, although it is said that his father was only an average
violinist, according to his contemporaries, and an occasional
composer. Like his sister, who played the piano from an
exceptionally early age, little Wolfgang was a child prodigy. It is
said that already at the age of six he was able to compose music
- much to the joy of his father. Some of the notes in his earliest
compositions are hidden under big blotches of ink, for the
young composer had not yet mastered the art of using the ink
pot, dipping into it too often.

The happy father would take his children around to
concerts, where they astonished the audience with their flawless
performance. At the age of six, for instance, Mozart gave his first
concert in Vienna, the seat of the Hapsburg monarchy. By then
he could not only play the piano, but also the violin and organ.
His fame spread so fast and far that he was asked to perform for
the Empress Maria Theresia herself. This opened the door for
him to the homes aristocrats, noble palaces, where he would
dazzle everybody with his concert skills. Next, the father took
the children for a tour of Germany and France, where the
compositions of little Mozart came out in print for the first time.
The same was repeated in England, where Wolfgang Amadeus
composed six piano sonatas. Then he went to Italy, the promised
land of the opera genre. After his tour of Italy, Mozart was
a name that was monumentally famous all over Europe.

The first meeting of the Dušek family and Mozart took place
during the couple's postponed honeymoon visit to the
grandparents of the bride, the Weisers, who lived in Salzburg.
Although the Dušeks had married on October 21, 1776, in
Prague, they took this trip the following year. Since František
Xaver Dušek was a music composer and teacher himself, it is
a small wonder that the two should meet in Salzburg. Young
Amadeus was all for the friendship. A lover of women all his
life, he immediately joined the number of the admirers of the
voice and suitors of the beauty of graceful Josephine. It is likely
that the Dušeks invited Mozart to Prague right then.

But ten long years would pass before Mozart would actually come to Prague. Through those years, there would be occasional correspondence exchanges between the Dušeks and Mozart. Meanwhile, Mozart got married, on August 4, 1782, at St. Stephen's Cathedral in Vienna. His bride was Maria Constance Cecilia Josepha Johanna Weber (1762 - 1842). Six children were born to the couple, but only two of them lived to adulthood: two sons, Karl Thomas and Franz Xaver Wolfgang.

Mozart arrived to Prague for the first time on January 11, 1787, and stayed two months. During that visit, he did not meet with Josephine Dušek at all, because she had a concert engagement in Berlin. Mozart moved into a prestigious inn in Old Town Prague, *Na Nové hospodě* [New Inn], which later came to be known as hotel *U Zlatého anděla* [Golden Angel], in house No. 558 in Celetná Street, near *Prašná brána* [Powder Gate]. Another famous legend about Mozart is linked to this hotel in Prague. One evening, as Mozart was having dinner with his Prague friends, the door in the inn opened and in walked a street musician and harpist, Josef Häusler, alias Copánek [Little Ponytail], after the manner he tied his hair on the back of his neck. He was a well-known and popular figure in Prague. To amuse the guests, little anticipating with whom he had the honor, he picked up his instrument and started to play an aria from Mozart's *The Marriage of Figaro* and then another variation of the same tune. Mozart was astonished over the beautiful pure tones he played. He interrupted his dinner and praised the street artist publicly. Mozart used his time on Prague to conduct his opera, *The Marriage of Figaro*, at Stavovské Theater as well as a concert performance at the same theater.

The second time Mozart visited Prague was still in the same year, in October, and he stayed until mid-November. This time over, he stayed in house No. 420, called *U Tří lvíčků* [Three Little Lions] at Uhelný trh [Coal Market] in Old Town Prague. During this second stay, he composed and completed his opera *Don Giovanni*. A plaque commemorates the visit of the music genius in the house. From there, Mozart was very close to Stavovské Theater and could also be constantly in touch with his librettist, Lorenzo da Ponte, who was staying in hotel *Platýz* [Flounder] on the opposite side of the street. Mozart would sometimes go to play billiard in an inn called *U Šturmů* in a street called *Skořepka*. During this time he happily accepted an invitation from the Dušeks who lived in a villa called *Bertramka* in Malá Strana, which he thus made famous forever. Even A. Schurig, a German writer, wrote at one point: "Bertramka should be called Mozart's home. It would deserve it much more that his places in Salzburg or Vienna." Today, the former country estate features Mozart's frequently visited monument. It was here that he wrote his famous opera aria, on November 3, 1787, called *Bella mia fiamma addio*. The composition of this famous aria, which he had been promising to write for a long time, is accountable to a little trick. The trick was played on him by Josephine Dušek who took Mozart to a garden pavilion which used to stand there, where all the writing tools and paper were already prepared on a table. She then locked the door and would not release him until the piece was written. When done, Mozart had one condition: he said he would tear the music sheet to pieces immediately, unless Josephine Dušek could sing the whole part without making a mistake. This she was able to do and so the aria was spared.

During this visit to Prague, Mozart also visited, on November 16, 1787, the Premonstrate Monastery on Strahov. In the Strahov Abbey Cathedral of the Ascension of Virgin Mary, he improvised on the organ. Exactly 200 years later, a marble plaque and a monumental bronze bust of Mozart was unveiled in the Abbey to commemorate the event. Mozart also visited the Monastery and Hospital of Charity Brothers, *Na Františku*, in Old Town Prague, where he played on the spinet (harpsichord). Then he visited the St. Simon and Judith Church, which formed a part of the Monastery, and played the organ to a great joy of the people who happened to be in the church. But the most important Mozart's activity during that visit was the world premiere of his opera *Don Giovanni* at Stavovské Theater. Mozart rehearsed the opera exhaustively, both with the orchestra and the singers, and he also conducted it himself during the premiere and four subsequent performances.

During his third visit, in April 1789, Mozart was practically just passing through Prague, staying only one afternoon and evening, spending the night in a hotel on Malá Strana, called *U Zlatého jednorožce* [Golden Unicorn]. He met only with František Xaver Dušek, because Josephine Dušek had left shortly before for Dresden. Upon leaving Prague, Mozart went in the same direction, crossing Dresden and Leipzig, he went to

Berlin, to the court of the Prussian king Friedrich II. His concerts there were very successful, but he turned down the King's offer to be his Court orchestra master for a generous salary, because he did not want to give up living in Vienna. He passed through Prague again on his way from Berlin back to Vienna at the beginning of May in the same year.

The fifth and last time that Mozart came to Prague was in August 1791. The Bohemian burghers had commissioned a gala opera from Mozart on the occasion of the coronation of Emperor Leopold II to the Bohemian throne. Historic records state that the commission arrived very late, but Mozart obliged anyway, having so little time for it that he was still composing in the stagecoach on his way to Prague. The coronation opera, whose plot is set in Ancient Rome, was titled *La clemenza di Tito*. This opera, too, had its world and Prague premiere at Stavovské Theater, on September 6, 1791. On leaving Prague that September, Mozart found it very hard to part with Prague and his many friends there, as if he anticipated that he would never return. The world-famous composer Wolfgang Amadeus Mozart died on December 5, 1791, in Vienna and was also buried there.

On December 14 in the same year, an in memoriam mass was served at the St. Mikuláš Cathedral in Prague, attended by 3,000 people. The program also included A. Rössler's *Requiem*, which featured a solo soprano part, sung by none other than Josephine Dušek. A symbolic catafalque was placed in the middle of the Cathedral, with the students from the Malá Strana High School standing along its sides as honor guards, wearing mourning sashes and holding burning torches. After the pious act ended, the bells of St. Mikuláš would ring, joined by the bells of all the churches in Prague.

Al. von Saar: A View of Charles Bridge and a part of Old Town
from Kampa Island, 1881, oil (Vienna - State Gallery)

Niccolo

$\mathcal{P}$AGANINI

The Nostitz Theater in Prague, later renamed after its new owner to Stavovské, was built as an antipode to the Viennese *Hof- und Nationaltheater* and has collected a wealth of memories over the more than 200 years of its existence. Hundreds of artists, musicians, actors, and dancers have performed on its stage. While many of them have dropped into oblivion, the performances and engagements of others are rightfully the pride of Stavovské Theater to this day. Among the most prominent performers, there certainly stands out the Italian composer and, above all, world-famous violinist, Niccolo Paganini (1782 - 1840). Even today, his performance is synonymous with absolute perfection.

Niccolo Paganini was born on October 27, 1782, in Genoa, Italy, in a relatively poor family. His father, Antonio Paganini, was a stevedore in the port, where he later became a clerk. His mother, Teresa, born Bocciardi, had a great talent for singing. Antonio Paganini also had a talent - he was a self-taught violinist. Niccolo's parents often went out in the evening and performed in the Genoa port pubs to earn some extra money for their meager living.

Fortunately, the parents were aware of their son's extraordinary gift for music and they did their best to let him take violin lessons. Not only did little Niccolo make a very quick progress, he could also play without a music sheet almost instantly. The next years of little Niccolo's life corresponded with the Napoleonic wars. First, his father took him to Florence, then to Parma, to let him get an education with a better - but also more expensive - teacher each time. The investment was soon to return, for as soon as Niccolo Paganini began to give concerts, his fame spread all over Northern Italy in no time at all. His phenomenal memory enabled him to play even the hardest compositions of famous composers by heart. Moreover, he also started to compose music.

At that time, he was given a truly royal present: a French merchant and music lover, Pierre Livron, gave him a magnificent concert instrument, a violin made by Guarneri, which connoisseurs consider superior even to Stradivari. For this gift, Paganini had to promise his patron that he would never let anyone else play the violin. The promise was kept, not only during Paganini's life, but also after his death, when his Guarneri violin was put in the Genoa Museum and silenced forever.

Paganini's star ascended to very great heights - his devilishly brilliant technique was simply unrivalled, as his admirers liked to claim. His concerts were attended by the cream of society wherever he went. He was frequently asked to perform in the palaces of aristocrats. Moving about in that kind of circle allowed him to establish numerous amorous connections and affairs with ladies from the highest places. Thus he also learned the more private side of his audiences' favor. During a concert in Ferrara, he was to perform with a famous soprano Marchini. But the diva cancelled at the last moment and, as an emergency solution, was understudied by a singer with an inadequately trained voice. But the audience would not have it, trying to whistle the young singer off the stage. Paganini sent her away and started to create all kinds of animal sounds on his violin, sounds like dog barking, hen cackling, pig grunting, etc. But when he - in the direction of those who had whistled - used his G string to produce a sound that was indiscernible from the braying of a donkey, the audience got the point and stormed the stage, and Paganini was lucky to have managed to escape in time. He never again performed in Ferrara.

In 1822 - though some sources claim it happened a year later - Paganini met Antonia Bianchi in Venice, who became his common-law wife for several years and gave birth to his son, whom they named Achillin. Paganini adored his son, but the relationship with his son's mother had developed many problems, once the initial infatuation was over. The Maestro's biographers took a very harsh position towards her. It is said that she was superficial, stubborn, cynical, and a liar, too. Things came to a head in Vienna, in 1828, where the couple parted for good. The violin Maestro paid out his son in cash, including a previously arranged and now increased lump-sum alimony for the mother.

On his way from Vienna, Paganini made a short stopover at the castle *Hradec u Opavy* for a little rest and then he went to Karlovy Vary [Carlsbad] for a short spa visit. But the famous West Bohemian spa did not improve the state of his health very much and so when, on October 4, 1828, Paganini arrived in Prague with his three-year-old son Achillin, he was not in very good shape. They stayed at the hotel *U Černého koně* [Black Horse Inn], which used to stand across from *Prašná brána* [Powder Gate]. Paganini is said not to have had suitcases or travel baskets when he traveled. Instead, he would have several violin cases containing his clothing and personal things. In his hotel room, he used to make an incredible mess, but would not allow the service personnel to tidy it up.

At first, due to his poor health, there was no point in trying to arrange any concert engagements. What's more, he suffered from a painful inflammation of the gums which soon developed into a full-blown case of periostitis. He had to undergo a complicated operation - not just one but two, one after the other. The first surgery was done on October 10, the subsequent one on November 4. The second procedure probably resulted in his losing all his lower teeth. For this reason, he could not eat anything but liquid food. Concerts were out of the question for at least several more weeks, nor was he fit enough to receive any visitors. To make things worse, he came down with a severe throat infection.

By the end of November, the health of the Italian violin

virtuoso had finally improved so that, on December 1, 1828, he was able to give his first concert in Prague at the Stavovské Theater. The price of the tickets was five times higher than usual. Witty Pragonians were quick to christen the five-piece coin a "paganinka." The most expensive tickets cost 20 guilders of conventional currency, the lowest price was 1 guilder. Despite the price, the concert sold out, with the exception of a few seats. The program of the concert was segmented into 3 parts, whereby each part contained 3 music compositions. Of course, there had to be a Mozart, his overture to the *Magic Flute*, and Paganini's *Military Sonata in G-major*.

The second concert took place three days later, on December 4, 1828. The theater was a little less full, which meant that, in accordance with the terms of the contract, the artist was paid a little less than before. Again, the program was arranged in three parts, with 3 compositions in each. After the concert, the press issued the first reviews - mostly positive ones. The critic's pen was also held by Julius Max Schottky, who was known for his historical and topographical work on Prague, and who then published, in 1830, a book written in a so-called compilation method and titled *Paganini's Leben und Treiben*, [Paganini's Life and Work] with the artist's portrait by G. Döbler and the following motto: "I do not fear greatness and I do have but contempt for mediocrity."

Another Paganini concert, the third one, took place on December 9, 1828, at the Stavovské Theater, again. His co-performers were Kateřina Podhorská, soprano, and Sebastian Binder, tenor. This time, the proceeds of the concert were to go to the benefit of the Asylum for the Poor of the capital city of Prague, whose chairman was Count Karel Anselm Thurn Taxis. The program of the concert was arranged in the same manner, as were the programs of all the subsequent concerts, which were attended by a lesser number of viewers. This was due primarily to the ticket prices. The fourth Paganini concert, held on December 13, 1828, once again at Stavovské Theater, drew even fewer listeners. Contemporary reviews stated that the Maestro appeared to be in a good physical condition, after what he had been forced to endure in the previous months.

His fifth concert, on December 16, 1828, was presented - for commercial reasons - as his last one. The attendance was lower, again, which was at that time attributed to rumors which had begun to circulate in Prague. Paganini was, as the rumors claimed, a very stingy man who allegedly murdered his mistress and had been jailed for it for many years. This proves that no one is safe before the wagging tongues of slanderers, so even Paganini, like many others, who achieved so much in their lives, became a victim of defamation. After the fifth and last concert, the sixth one could not be called anything but a farewell concert. It was held on December 20, 1828, at Stavovské Theater, like all the previous ones. As an encore, Paganini played his transcription of Haydn's *Anthem of Austrian Nations*, without the accompaniment of an orchestra.

In the tally of the accounts which followed, the overall revenues from all six of Paganini's concerts amounted to 5,360 guilders of co nventional currency, which - if averaged and compared with his concerts in Vienna - was considerably less than for his Viennese performances. One of the reasons may have been the aforementioned prices which were responsible for lower attendance, but we must also realize that Prague was a provincial town, compared to Vienna, the seat of the Imperial monarchy.

Paganini and his son spent Christmas 1828 in Prague. He left by postal coach on January 12, 1829, for Dresden and Leipzig, where he was to give concerts. On the day of his departure from Prague, he wrote a power-of-attorney for Prof. Julius Max Schottky, the text of which was: "I, the undersigned hereby grant a permission to Mr. Prof. Schottky to publish my biography, and I implore him to do everything in his power to defend me and quash the libel committed against me by my enemies. Prague, January 12, 1829. Niccolo Paganini."

The wizard on the violin, Italian virtuoso Niccolo Paganini, died at 5 o'clock p.m. on May 27, 1840, in Nice, France. According to his testament, his son, Achillin Paganini, was his universal heir, inheriting all the Maestro's musical instruments and compositions, but smaller monetary sums were also willed to other members of his family.

In closing this *Paganini in Prague* chapter, let us mention some great past Bohemian violinists. First of all, there was Josef Slavík (1806 - 1833), nicknamed "Czech Paganini". The great Maestro himself was so enthused by his performance that he declared:: "When you play, the world shakes!" Some time later, when Paganini's son Achillin heard the performance of a Bohemian violin virtuoso František Ondříček (1857 - 1922), he called out: "I recognize the bow of my father!" To demonstrate how much he admired his music performance, he had Paganini's crypt opened so Ondříček could pay homage to the Maestro. A screw that accidentally fell from it became Ondříček's talisman which he carried in his violin case for the rest of his life. The music section of the National Museum has in its collections not only a letter from Paganini, but also a symbolic golden key to Paganini's coffin. The last distinguished Czech violinist to receive this supreme prize as an award for masterly performance was Jan Kubelík (1880 - 1940).

Entrance to Kotce in Prague, about 1820, watercolor (Prague - Municipal Museum)

Peter

PARLER

A Bull of Pope Clement VI, dated April 30, 1344, elevates the ancient Diocese of Prague, established in 973, to an Archdiocese, at the impulse of the King of Bohemia, John Luxembourg, and his son, Charles, Margrave of Moravia, a former Pope's disciple during the Pope's youth at the French Royal Court. This instituting act exempts the Prague Diocese and, by extension, the Olomouc Diocese, from affiliation with the clerical province of Mayen and annexes them to metropolitan Prague. The first Archbishop of Prague was Arnošt of Pardubice.

The ruler of the Bohemian lands, King John Luxembourg, his son Charles, and Archbishop Arnošt of Pardubice - in the presence of many secular and clerical dignitaries - ceremoniously laid the foundation stone of the future St. Vitus Cathedral at the Prague Castle. This took place on November 21, 1344, according to a relatively contemporary document, a transcript from a chronicle, written by a chronographer, spiritual man, and, later on, the third director of the cathedral's construction, Beneš Krabice of Weitmil.

Even before the end of his father's reign, Charles IV summoned to Prague the architect and builder Matthias of Arras, who thus became historically the first builder of the cathedral. His design was a sober structure in the French Gothic style, a three-bay basilica, cathedral type. Charles IV tried to influence the overall concept of the structure, including the details, but Matthias of Arras was not to be the man who would satisfy the grandiose ideas of the King. His bust in the triforium of the St. Vitus Cathedral bears the following inscription: „Matthias of Arras, a French town, the first master and builder of this Church, whom King Charles the Fourth, at that time also Margrave of Moravia, later crowned a Roman King in Avignon, was brought to this land to build this Church, and directed the construction of this Church from 1344 until 1352 AD, the year he died." Let us add that either the date or the title of King Charles IV must be wrong because Charles IV became Roman Emperor, as a counter-candidate of Ludwig of Bavaria, only several weeks before the Battle of Crecy, where John Luxembourg died, on July 11, 1346.

After Matthias of Arras died, the construction continued for some time according to the pre-existing plans. But a project of such magnitude needed a new building master. With a great foresight, Charles IV appointed a certain Peter Parler (1333 - 1399), who was only 23 years old. It was this man whose name is written in the history of the Cathedral in golden script, as it was his architectural skills and creative talent which deserve the largest share of credit for the completion of this magnificent structure.

Peter Parler was born in Swabian Gmünd, or his parents had settled there when he was still very young. The inscription in the triforium, next to Parler's bust, states that his father, Heinrich Parler of Cologne on the Rhine, was a foreman in Schwabian Gmünd. His name carried a professional meaning, suggesting someone who supervises other workers - and such was his father's position when the cathedral was built in Cologne on the Rhine. The father was a founder of a prominent Parler dynasty of builders and masons. The members of the family worked on many, mostly sacral, structures throughout Europe. They used the same master brand symbol or emblem: a masonry double-angled bar.

The most famous member of the family, Peter Parler, came

to Prague probably in 1356, although earlier sources claim that it may have been a little before that date. It is possible that Charles IV originally wanted to hire his father, who however recommended that he take his son. He probably provided his son, before he left, with plans, both for masonry and architecture, which were passed down from generation to generation and constituted the greatest treasures of the family. Charles IV may had the foresight to take the son due to his age, because a construction of the size he had in mind could not be completed in one man's life, so he obviously wanted one builder to carry on as long as possible.

Upon acquainting himself thoroughly with Matthias' work, Peter Parler set out to work with great enthusiasm. His predecessor had left behind solid foundations, the chancel, eight chapels of polygonal shape, and attached thereto was a gallery with arcades for the choir, but the St. Wenceslaus Chapel, the most important one, architecturally and ideologically, had been barely begun. Let us recall, telegraphically, all that was completed after Peter Parler took over the construction: 1362 - sacristy is completed; 1367 - St. Wenceslaus Chapel, erected over the saint's grave pursuant to the King's concept, is completed and, on Nov. 30, 1367, consecrated; 1368, July 9 - Southern Portal (Porta aurea) consecrated - the builder had it placed, like the main tower, in the southern side wall of the Cathedral, thus turning the Cathedral symbolically towards the King's palace and his city; 1370 - ring of chapels and the choir gallery up to triforium level are completed; 1370 - 1371 - mosaic over the Southern Portal is completed; 1371 - the upper choir gallery is begun; 1372 - the large snail stairway next to the southern cathedral bay is completed; 1373 - the triumphal arch and the arches of the side bays are completed; 1374 - 1375 - the triforium is completed; 1376 - eleven windows of the upper choir are completed; 1377 - upper support structure is begun; 1385 - the walls between the temporary bay and the upper choir come down; 1392 - the foundation stone for the three bays is laid; 1396 - large southern tower is begun.

A commendable amount of work for one human life, the life of a master of the ultimate Gothic style, Peter Parler. His avant-garde system of tracery vaults is being admired to this day by specialists and lovers of architecture. Peter Parler was the first architect who no longer split the vaults into isolated fields, so that the whole space underneath is topped with a system of short ribs forming a not very dense vault system. His talent in masonry and carving was, however, not inferior to his building skills, as numerous portrait busts in the triforium of the St. Vitus Cathedral and other of his creations demonstrate.

Simultaneously with the building of St. Vitus Cathedral, Peter Parler also managed the construction of the Stone Bridge. The foundation stone for this marvelous technical wonder of medieval building art, today called Charles Bridge, was laid on July 9, 1357. He also built the Staroměstská Mostecká Věž [Old Town Bridge Tower] which stands on the first pillar of the bridge and whose portal was a gate to Karlův most [Charles Bridge]. Considered the most beautiful medieval tower in Europe, decorated with outstanding works of sculpting art, the tower is to a large extent Peter Parler's work. As for other parts of Bohemia, let us not forget Parler's work on the choir gallery of St. Bartholomew in Cologne near Prague.

Peter Parler certainly deserved to become a wealthy Prague burgher. He received a substantial pay, in addition to numerous emoluments *in naturalia*. He owned a house at Hradčanské náměstí, No. 62, and he built another house, No. 177, in the place on Loretánská Street where Hrzánský Palace stands today. As his material standing improved, so did his position in the society. He became an alderman in Hradčany, for instance. Married twice, he had three sons with his first wife, Gertrud, of whom Václav and Jan followed the footsteps of their father and continued in the completion of the Cathedral, especially the big tower. The construction was interrupted in 1420, due to the Hussite wars. With his second wife, Elizabeth Anna of Boer, Parler had two more sons, Pavel and Janek.

The Prague Cathedral's historically second builder, Peter Parler, died on July 13, 1399, in Prague and is buried in the Cathedral next to his predecessor, Matthias of Arras. The place of his last repose was chosen by his sons, Václav and Jan, who also created the tombstone over his grave.

In 1928, as part of the completion works on the Cathedral, attributed to the merits of architect Kamil Hilbert, the interior of the Cathedral was subjected to major archeological research. For this purpose, the original paving of the old part of the Cathedral was lifted and redone. During this work that same year, in August, an extraordinary find was made. Near the northern wall of the sacristy, there stood a Baroque confessional. Underneath the confessional, there were two rectangular tombstones, each over 2 meters long. Since the confessional covered only about one half of the tombstones, the other halves were worn smooth. After shifting the confessional to the side, the unworn inscriptions on the other halves of the tombstone left no doubt that these were the graves of the first builders of the St. Vitus Cathedral, Matthias of Arras and Peter Parler.

The discovery of graves of such significance caused a sensation in Prague. The skeletons were examined by Professor Jindřich Matiegka and the textiles were passed on to other specialists for further research. The unworn inscriptions helped identify the exact dates on which the two famous builders died. A detailed report of the find of the grave of Matthias of Arras was sent by the Ministry of Education and Culture to relevant French scientists. The opening of the graves was filmed by A. B. Film Company and extensive photographic documentation was taken by the Štenc company.

On August10, 1929, the bodily remains of the famous builders, Matthias of Arras and Peter Parler, were buried in a dignified, new burial place in the Mary Magdalene Chapel, now called Valdštejnská, in the old part of the Cathedral, near the monument of St. Jan Nepomuk. The chapel was remodeled and a new altar was built on its frontal wall. Near the railing of the chapel is, to the left side, the grave of Matthias of Arras, and to the right, Peter Parler's. The original tombstones of the builders are set into the wall of the chapel, so the inscription would not be worn down by the feet of visitors any more. The lead coffins with the remains of the builders were lowered into openings in the red marble floor, and the openings are set into bronze frames. Steel plaques with inscriptions were placed inside. The coffins were covered with sashes bearing the seals of their donors, the Provost of the Diocese Chapter, Bishop Sedlák, architect Hilbert, and the St. Vitus Unity. Thus the remains of both builders, resting in silk-wrapped coffins, finally found much deserved eternal peace.

Antonín Pucherna: Garden in the former main Church Bay of
Virgin Mary's Under the Chains in Malá Strana, about 1820,
sepia colored pencil drawing, (Kutná Hora - Vocel Museum)

F. X. Sandmann: Prague-Malá Strana, about 1845, watercolor
(Prague - Municipal Museum)

August Friedrich

₽IEPENHAGEN

I n Michalská Street in Old Town Prague stands an ancient-looking house, No. 436, called *U Železných dveří* [Iron Gates]. The house has a passage from one street to another, from Michalská to Jilská. The passage goes through an irregularly shaped longish courtyard, where one may find a commemorative plaque, informing the visitor of the history of the building, certainly one of the most picturesque corners of Prague. Over the centuries, the house had many owners and even more tenants. Among the tenants who had left a deep trace which even time cannot wipe off, was the painter August Friedrich Piepenhagen (1791 - 1868).

He was born on August 2, 1791, in Solingen, Prussia. His father, Johann Ludwig Piepenhagen, operated a small button manufacture, and this was the trade that his son August had learned as well. As was common in those days, having learned a trade, the young man went abroad to learn the ways of the world as a button-maker and journeyman. The road took him to Switzerland where he met an aging painter, a master of his

trade, whom he asked to teach him paint. As Dr. Prokop Toman
states in his monumental *New Dictionary of Czechoslovak
Creative Artists*, that painter probably was Heinrich Wuest
(1741 - 1821) of Zurich. The impressions which he imprinted in
his memory at a young age, especially the beauty of the Alpine
nature, were a great inspiration to Piepenhagen in his later
career as an artist. But the road to the painter's palette is very
long, if one has to make a living, so he continued to make
buttons, too.

Piepenhagen came to Prague sometime between 1810 and
1811. He found work in the workshop of a button- and
trimming-maker, Jan Rissbitter, whose workshop was in house
No 436, *U Železných dveří*. During rare moments of leisure,
Piepenhagen would, from the beginning of his stay in Prague,
depict his beautiful memories of the romantic Swiss
countryside. But the cooperation of Master Rissbitter with his
journeyman did not last very long, because Jan Rissbitter died
on December 5, 1811. Piepenhagen was now faced with two
problems at once. For one, ahead of him loomed financial
problems, for the other, he had to decide whether or not he
would stay in Prague at all and try to pursue his newly
developed ambition in painting. He solved his problems in line
with the proverbial "killing two birds with one stone"; he took
over the operations of the workshop and soon thereafter
married the widow, Kateřina Rissbitter, born Měchura (* 23. 3.
1785). They married on November 29, 1815. The groom was
24 years old, or rather 24 years young, the bride was 6 years
older. The first years after the marriage the couple lived in the
house *U Železných dveří*. It is here that their three children
were born, one by one, from 1816 until 1825, three daughters in
all: Anna, who later married the well-known steel-carver Josef
Rybička (1817 - 1872), Karolina Ludmila, and Luisa. Both
younger daughters also became recognized painters.

As time went by, August Friedrich Piepenhagen began to
assert himself as a painter in Prague, painting mostly
landscapes. Beginning in 1822, he would send his work to
Prague art exhibitions; later he would even exhibit his work
abroad. In 1842 in Berlin, 1857 in Munich, and most often - in
1842, 1843, 1866, 1867, and 1868 - in Vienna. To refresh his
romantic view of landscapes, he would travel about Germany,
France, Switzerland, and Belgium. Though an autodidact, i.e.,

self-taught painter, who was inspired by the beauty of the nature and the rest he filled in from his imagination, he opened a private art school in Prague in 1836. His specialty were renditions of landscapes in different moods and shapes, mountainous sceneries, forests in stormy weather, and above all landscapes at night, in the light of the moon. Although his paintings were quite popular in Prague - and some of his works are in the collections of the National Gallery to this day - he continued to work as a trimming-maker, too. He used to say about his double career: "Art walks about, looking for bread, only to find it in trade."

In the Prague artistic scene, Piepenhagen made close friends with a well-known Bohemian painter Josef Navrátil (1798 - 1865), who, in his youth, like Piepenhagen, had learned a trade with his father to become an interior painter. He became an artist only later, during the years 1819 - 1823, when he visited Bergler's school of painting at the Prague Academy of Fine Arts. The friendship and mutual liking of both artists were extended into their family lives as well. For instance, Piepenhagen's wife Kateřina was Godmother at the christening of Josef Navrátil's daughter Kateřina on January 30, 1831.

We have mentioned that two of Piepenhagen's daughters, Karolina Ludmila (1821 - 1902) and Luisa (1825 - 1893), became painters. Both of them, more or less successfully, copied their father's artistic style. Of course, he was their first teacher, too. Luisa later went to Vienna to study painting formally, from 1874 to 1875. Karolina Ludmila participated in the Prague exhibitions of the *Krasoumná jednota* [Fine Arts Society]. In her last will and testament, she made a generous bequest: the substantial sum of 50,000 guilders, as well as the art works of her father, including sketches and drawing, she willed to a foundation named Mohr-Piepenhagen, which supports landscape-painting artists. By way of explanation, let us add that Karolina Ludmila had been married twice. First, she married Klement, a knight of Weyroth, then a colonel and free-born landowner, K. Mohr von Ehrenfeld.

Piepenhagen would spend the summers with his family on an estate known as *Jenerálka* near Divoká Šárka. The romance of the surrounding nature in that place was enough for inspiration, the rest he would make up from his imagination. It was at *Jenerálka*, too, that death found Piepenhagen. It happened on September 27, 1868. *Jenerálka*, formerly a country estate, was later rebuilt as a summer palace. Originally registered in the land register of Nebušice, it was transferred towards the end of the 1980's into the land register of Dejvice.

August Friedrich Piepenhagen was buried on September 30, 1868, at the Evangelical cemetery in Karlín. In 1870, his family had a dignified monument built over his grave, the work of sculptor Tomáš Seidan. But the Karlín cemetery, which had been founded in the second half of last century, was victim of a major catastrophe in 1890. The whole cemetery was flooded during that year's great flood and the cemetery was completed destroyed by water from the Vltava River. For this reason it was discussed that there would be no more burials there and the cemetery would be liquidated. The negotiations on the subject dragged on for several years so that the actual liquidation was begun only in 1894. Simultaneously, it was decided that the most prominent graves, including tombstones, would be carried to the Olšany cemetery. This is what was done to the grave and tombstone of August Friedrich Piepenhagen. His bodily remains were transferred to the 7th cemetery in Olšany, 12th section, grave No. 8. Moved along with him was also his daughter Luisa who had died on November 14, 1893, in Prague, and was buried at the Karlín cemetery. The bodily remains of Karolina Ludmila, who died on January 3, 1902, also in Prague, were buried in the family grave at Olšany.

In conclusion, let us mention that three exhibitions of the works of August Friedrich Piepenhagen were organized in memoriam of this painter. The first one took place in Prague in 1917, at the Rubeš Gallery in Prague, where 195 of his works were exhibited. The second one, in the same location, took place in 1935, and exhibited 60 of his works. Both these exhibitions featured also the paintings of his daughter Karolina Ludmila. The last comprehensive exposition of Piepenhagen's works took place under the patronage of the National Gallery at the break of 1960 - 1961, in Prague.

Al. Bubák: Holy Cross the Minor Chapel in Old Town Prague,
1864, originally a lithograph (Prague, National Museum)

Aug. Mathieu: The Stone (Charles) Bridge and Malá Strana,
about 1850, colored lithograph by Bichebois and Fichot,
„staffage" by Bayot (Prague - L. Sachs)

Josip

$\mathcal{P}$LEČNIK

When the independent Czechoslovak Republic was founded in 1918 and President T. G. Masaryk arrived at the Prague Castle, that stone symbol of statehood was in a very poor condition in general. The seat of many rulers had been Vienna, which left Prague, where all construction activities had ceased in the third quarter of the 18th century, to slowly decay. To improve the state of affairs, a Slovenian architect, named Josip Plečnik (1872 - 1957), who had been living in Prague since 1911 and was involved in pedagogical activities as a professor of architecture at the School of Industrial Arts, was called to help.

Josip Plečnik was born on January 23, 1872, in Ljubljana. He learned carpentry in his father's shop, but discovered his real interest and talent after he enrolled in a trade school in Graz. In the years 1894 - 1898 be studied at the Viennese Academy of Creative Arts in the studio of Professor Otto Wagner. During his studies at the Academy, he went on an academic trip to Italy.

After graduation, he stayed in Vienna where he developed several structural designs.

In 1910, Plečnik was invited to Prague by his professional colleague, friend, and one-time co-student - an avant-garde Czech architect, Jan Kotěra (1871 - 1923). A year later, Plečnik began to teach in Prague. During his teaching career, from 1911 until 1921, he trained a number of outstanding students and disciples of his architectural concepts. For the sake of an example, let us at least name architect Otto Rothmayer, who had collaborated with Plečnik on the reconstruction of the Prague Castle and continued with that work on his own later on. It was Kotěra who introduced Plečnik to T. G. Masaryk, the president of the new republic. In 1920, the President's Office commissioned Plečnik, who had won an architectural competition for a project involving the reconstruction of the dilapitated southern gardens in the Prague Castle, the *Rajská* and *Na Valech* gardens. At the recommendation of architect Jan Kotěra and the Mánes Association of Creative Artists, the President of the Republic appointed Josip Plečnik to the position of Chief Architect of the Prague Castle.

Although Plečnik's architectural, urban designer, and creative capabilities were unquestionable, as he had demonstrated by all his work, a wave of criticism arose against this appointment. In the first place, there were objections to the fact that one of the symbols of Czech statehood, the Prague Castle, was to be remodeled by a foreigner. The conservatives criticized the very idea of remodeling the Castle's ancient palaces in any radical manner. But during his 15 years at the Castle, Plečnik demonstrated not only that he had extraordinary creative courage, but also a great portion of humbleness. Having acquainted himself with the history and traditions, he carefully made various impressions of modernist and democratic spirit in the individual parts of the Castle.

Plečnik completed the entrance from Hradčanské náměstí to the southern gardens and the enormous cascade stairs to *Rajská zahrada* [Paradise Garden], topping the reconstruction project with a huge basin of Mrákotín granite. During the transport to its destination, the movers had to employ military technology, and the transport was followed by crowds of onlookers. The Baroque fountain which used to stand at that spot was moved to the *Na Valech* Garden. In this garden,

Plečnik lowered the whole length of the support wall from the 19th century, thus opening a beautiful panorama of Prague from the main garden path. Extensive landscaping was carried out and the Moravian bastion and pavilion Bellevue were completed. Plečnik connected the southern gardens with the third courtyard of the Castle by so-called Bull Stairs.

The Slovenian architect was particularly successful with the remodeling of the Castle's interiors. The entrance hall with columns reaching up through the three storeys of the frontal wing is most highly praised. Also the adaptation of the private apartments of the President, featuring an entrance hall and a winding staircase, is noteworthy. A great philosopher, as T. G. Masaryk certainly was, a monumental library was an absolute must. In accordance with the President's explicit wishes, his own apartments, situated in the southern and central wing of the New Palace, were remodeled very inconspicuously, with emphasis on functionality.

Plečnik also designed and supervised the reconstruction of the Castle's courtyards and repaving. Before this could be done, however, an extensive archeological survey had to be carried out, especially in the 3rd courtyard. In 1928, as part of the remodeling works and in connection with the placement of a large monolith of local origin, the workers removed a Baroque fountain situated near the statue of St. George on a horse (the statue of the legendary saint in a fight with a dragon dates back to 1373) and replaced it with a tall edged pillar - the statue was then put back in its place. Josip Plečnik proposed to make a shallow water reservoir, set into the ground, with a railing around it.

In the vicinity of the monument, he had a massive granite monolith erected, measuring 15 meters in height. It is one of many Plečnik's creative ideas which enrich the Castle's environment to this day. The granite monolith, shaped like an obelisk, was brought in 1923 from the Mrákotín quarry situated at the foot of the highest hill of the Bohemian-Moravian Highlands, Javořice. The transport of roughly 112 tons of the stone structure was a difficult task and sensation in its time. As a matter of fact, the first attempt ended in a failure, because the first obelisk broke in half. With the second effort the operation was a success. The placement of the obelisk was debated for a while. There were suggestions to put it in different locations, including the Old Town Square, but Plečnik followed his artistic intuition and had the monolith placed in the 3rd court yard at the Castle, against the background of a low-height Diocese building, where the contrast of heights gives the location a visual symbolism. The monolith was ceremoniously installed in 1928, on the occasion of the 10th anniversary of independent Czechoslovakia.

On the first courtyard, the place of prime importance, near the Matthias Gate, Plečnik had two big flag posts installed. They are formed out of two 30-meter spruce threes from Moravian woods. He categorically refused to have iron or concrete pillars made for this purpose, giving preference, according to his own words, to the most beautiful trees of local origin.

Despite his enormous work load, Plečnik accepted an offer in 1921 from his native Ljubljana to teach architecture at a newly founded Technical University, and he also managed to actively participate in the architectural reconstruction of the President's residence, the summer palace in Lány. On this project, too, he designed a number of impressive architectural elements, whereby made a particularly attractive use of the presence of water.

But this account of his activities does not by far cover all his accomplishments in Prague. He also worked on monumental sacral architecture in Královské Vinohrady, at today's Náměstí Jiřího z Poděbrad, where he built a parish church named Nejsvětějšího Srdce Páně [Holiest Heart of the Lord]. His design was chosen out of among 31 bidders in a public tender called in 1919. For financial reasons, the actual construction of the original project took place 1929 - 1932. The church's characteristic facade of glazed bricks, combined with blocks of artificial granite, is dominated by a 42-meter-tall tower whose width spans the entire width of the structure. The wider side walls of the tower, there is a glass clock with a dial measuring 7.6 meters in diameter. The inside of the church is made of fine-finish bare bricks. The construction of the church was officially begun on August 19, 1929, by the Abbot of the Strahov Abbey, P. Method Zavoral, and the consecration was carried out on May 8, 1932, by the Archbishop of Prague, Cardinal Dr. Karel Kašpar.

During his stay in Prague and, of course, during his work on the Prague Castle, Plečnik maintained a close friendship and also some emotional ties to Masaryk's daughter, Alice Masaryk

(1879 - 1966), as their correspondence preserved to this day testifies. After her mother's death, Alice Masaryk, a long-term chairperson of the Czechoslovak Red Cross, essentially became mistress of the Castle and complemented her father's role, as if she were the first lady of the country. Plečnik's activities in Prague ended in 1935, when a wave of protests against the implementation of any of his projects at the Castle or its vicinity in the future arose, on the part of professional colleagues and other specialists. What's more, he lost support for his ambitious projects when the President of the Republic, T. G. Masaryk, abdicated on December 14, 1935, due to his failing health.

To illustrate the atmosphere of those days, let us quote a passage from a letter written to the Club of Old Prague in that year: "The Czechoslovak women beseech the Club of Old Prague, known for its beneficial activities for the salvation of historic monumental treasures of Czechoslovakia, to use it influence and energetically stop efforts to alter the appearance of the nation's dearest treasure, *Hradčany* and its surroundings, lest the nation be bound to lose its most beautiful panorama, so familiar to us as well as many people in distant foreign lands. We have so many outstanding architects of our own who are able, emotionally attached, and patriotic enough to carry out the necessary repairs without spoiling the inheritance we have from out ancestors. What not even any of our enemies managed to destroy in the past, is now being destroyed by an architect of foreign descent, in an alien style, without love or feeling for our historic treasures. The women of Czechoslovakia plead: Save out Hradčany for our children, so they would not stand before the ruined Castle accusing us and judge us for having done nothing to save it." The letter was signed by 245 persons.

The architect of global fame, Josip Plečnik, returned to his native Ljubljana and continued his activities in various parts of Slovenia. He participated in legislative matters, built churches, schools, and palaces, designed monuments for the victims of the war, and crypts. His last work is probably the circular columnar pavilion for the President of Yugoslavia, Josip Brož Tito, in Brioni, in 1956. Death found Josip Plečnik on September 29, 1957.

From May 24 to 29, 1996, an exhibition was organized in Prague in his honor, titled Josip Plečnik - Architecture for New Democracy. The main organizer was the Prague Castle

Administration, under the patronage of President of the Czech Republic, Václav Havel, and President of Slovenia, Milan Kučan. The exhibition also featured some complementary activities and events, including several professional seminars. The event enjoyed an extraordinary amount of attention from the public, professional and non-professional alike. A documentary film titled "My Master" was made about this ingenious architect, by film director Pavel Koutský. On May 24, 1996, a short mass was given by the Archbishop of Prague, Cardinal Miloslav Vlk, at Plečnik's Cathedral in Vinohrady. The mass was concluded by a concert of the Madrigalists of Ljubljana from Slovenia.

Rudolf Alt: Týnský chrám with Krocín Fountain, oil, 1843 (from the collection of Konopiště Castle)

Auguste

RODIN

T he name of this giant of French sculpture is pronounced
all over the world with an undertone of respect for his
life-work. But both the life and work of Auguste
Rodin (1840 - 1917) had to endure and overcome many
obstacles, before achieving worldwide recognition. Born on
November 12, 1840, in Paris, in the family of an assistant clerk at
the police prefecture, he spent his childhood and youth in
relatively poor environment. Refusing to work with his father, he
won his parents' permission to study decorative arts. But his
repeated applications for admission to the Academy if Fine Arts,
were only to be rejected over and over again. He was a student
of Lecoq, after all, who was not well-liked, to put it mildly, and
there was therefore little motivation to Rodin a chance.

Rodin decided to follow the example of his sister who had
entered a convent with a broken heart. After a year in
a monastery he had an in-depth discussion with the superior
and returned to civilian life. He created his first magnificent
piece of work - *Man with a Broken Nose* - but was rejected.

To supplement his meager existence, he hired himself out as an assistant in the studio of sculptor Carrie-Belleuse whose work was very much "in" at that time. Thus he worked on commercial orders for several years, without any artistic invention at all. Perhaps the only plus of that period of his life was that he acquired a lot of skills in sculpting as a routine. When he finally parted with his employer, on ill terms, he accepted an offer to work with a Belgian sculptor Van Rasbourg. This opened the door for him to become creative on his own. During his visit to Italy, he was immensely impressed on seeing Michelangelo's David with his own eyes. He decided that he, too, would devote his time to sculpting male figures.

He created a nude sculpture, which he called *The Defeated*. It is the figure of a man leaning on a walking stick, lifting the other hand as if in silent protest. But criticism was so crushing that Rodin wanted to break the sculpture to pieces. Fortunately, he listened to his friends' advice, took the walking stick away and renamed it *The Age of Bronze*. Although rejected both by professional and amateur critics, he continued to pursue his own artistic concepts. He submitted a bid on Byron's monument in London, a National Defense Monument in Paris, but his works found no sympathy. The first piece that was partially accepted in 1878 was a nude male figure representing John the Baptist, under the condition that the particular part of his body would be covered with a fig leaf.

Shortly thereafter he accepted a commission to create the portal for the new Museum of Decorative Arts, which he never finished, although it is considered to be his life-work. He got very much involved in a commission from the city of Calais which wanted to build a monument to its citizens who had let themselves be captured in 1374, by the King of England, Edward III, to save the besieged city from occupation and massacre. There was also a monument for the Pantheon, of the French writer Victor Hugo, whom Rodin conceived as a nude man sitting at the sea... The matter ended with a scandal. Even the monument of another famous French writer, Honoré de Balzac, he first conceived as a nude figure, but then - mercifully and of his own impulse- wrapped him in a long cloak as was characteristic for the writer. During his work on this statue, he created 22 studies of Balzac's head, in a relatively short time,

8 studies in the nude, and 16 sketches of the cloak and draperies that he later put on the writer.

The determining point in Rodin's life was his participation at the World Exposition which took place in 1889 in Paris. He had a pavilion built near the exposition area, where he exhibited 170 of his works. At first, there was much hesitation, but gradually the reactions of the visitors became more spontaneously appreciative and interest grew, as did Rodin's satisfaction later. His pavilion was visited by many people, professionals and laymen alike, and Rodin became famous. Leaving evaluation of his work to the more competent, let us at least remind you of some of his world-famous works: *The Kiss*, *Eve*, and *The Thinker*.

Naturally, word of the famous sculptor got as far as Prague, too. Political and cultural relations between Paris and Prague were very intensive, after all, and so were artistic relations between the French and Bohemian creative scene. Many Bohemian artists spent time in Paris. Let us mention some names specifically, such as Zdenka Brauner, Luděk Marold, Václav Brožík, Alfonse Mucha, Jan Dědina, and Josef Mařatka. The last of the above named, the young sculptor Mařatka, Myslbek's student, went to Paris in 1900, on a scholarship and with the help of his supporter, architect and builder Josef Hlávka, to study in Rodin's studio where he had the honor of working for the Master. Rodin became very fond of his Bohemian student. Another famous name linked to Rodin was the poet Rainer Maria Rilke, born in Prague, who at one point worked for Rodin as his secretary.

The realization of Rodin's exhibition in Prague, in 1902, was possible thanks to the following events. First, it was the anniversary of Victor Hugo's birth in Paris to which an official delegation was sent from Prague. As part of its rich cultural program, the delegation also visited Rodin's studio. Rodin promised he would lend some of his sculptures and drawings for an exhibition in Prague. The credit for this promise goes to - and this was the second event - the Master's favorite assistant, Josef Mařatka. A useful idea was born, but a lot of work had to be done to make it a reality.

The work on the logistics of Rodin's exhibition in Prague was assumed by the Mánes Association of Creative Artists, of which Mařatka was a member. The driving element in the

Association was its chairman and sculptor, Stanislav Sucharda, who made sure that the preparatory committee was also joined by the representatives of the city of Prague and the town of Smíchov, still an independent suburban community at that time. The participation of the latter official was particularly important, because it was on his property, near the Kinský Palace, that an exhibition pavilion was built, in a record time of three weeks, designed and supervised by architect Jan Kotěra. The responsibility of the extensive correspondence concerning all the concrete organizational matters involved, and the number of art works to be shown, sat entirely on the shoulders of Stanislav Sucharda in Prague and Josef Mařatka in Paris.

Finally, the big day arrived: on May 10, 1902, Rodin's exhibition in Prague was to begin. Ceremonious speeches were given by JUDr. Karel Groš, the mayor of Prague, and Stanislav Sucharda, chairman of the Mánes Association. The visitors could view 88 completed sculptures and studies and several dozen of the Master's drawings. The prologue to the exhibition which appeared in the catalogue was written by F. X. Šalda, who called it *The Mother Tongue of a Genius*. The implication was, of course, that to express himself in sculpture was to Rodin like speaking his mother tongue. The poster for the exhibition was designed by Vladimír Županský, and the engraving on the invitation was created by Max Švabinský himself.

Auguste Rodin arrived in Prague by train on Wednesday, May 28, 1902. He was greeted at the railway station by Josef V. Novák, Imperial Alderman and member of a delegation from the City Hall of Prague. A short drive through the city followed, ending at Hotel Central in Hybernská Street where Rodin was to be housed. After a demanding journey, Rodin wished to take a good long break before attending to his demanding schedule in Prague.

On his second day in Prague, Rodin visited his exhibition in the pavilion near Kinský Gardens, but he did so only unofficially, incognito, so to speak. He wanted to do that to see it in peace and without being disturbed, so as to be able to have a true impression of it. That evening, he attended a reception at the Old Town City Hall, which was also attended by many prominent personages, including the French Consul. Subsequently, he visited the Municipal Museum. He also saw the library at the Strahov Abbey and the Prague Castle.

Friday, May 30, 1902, was the day of the official opening of the exhibition. It took place in the morning, around 10 o'clock. Rodin arrived in a coach car, in the company of Stanislav Sucharda. He was greeted by many people, among them also in French by Arnošt Hofbauer, a painter, graphic artist, and representative of young Bohemian artists. After viewing the exhibition, the visitors were invited to a banquet in Rodin's honor at Hotel Central. In the evening, the artist, accompanied by a number of people, went to the National Theater. Some sources claim that *The Bartered Bride* was on the program for the evening, others claim it was *Dalibor*. However, on the National Theater's repertoire for the 1901-1902 season, there were no operas at all. The new staging of the opera Dalibor was rehearsed only in the subsequent season, according to the program, and was performed from May 14, 1903, to February 22, 1910. Be it as it may, it is certain that after the performance at the National Theater, Rodin must have spent a few pleasant moments in the company of his new Prague friends, members of the *Mánes Association of Creative Artists*.

On Saturday, May 31, another banquet was organized at Hotel Central. Rodin also visited a colorful party at Queen Anne's summer palace, which was organized in memoriam to honor Bohemian poet and prose writer, Julius Zeyer. The proceeds from that event were to be used for the Zeyer' monument in Chotkovy Sady. Several photographs from that social event were published in *Zlatá Praha* magazine. Apart from his official program, Rodin also paid some private visits to certain people, such as professor Stanislav Sucharda, who gave him two small sculptures of his own, called *Lullaby* and *Wind*. It is said that he also visited, in the company of Zdenka Brauner, the famous Brauner's Mill in Roztoky. Another semi-private event, although in the company of several friends, was a small outing on a steam boat to Zbraslav, where he saw the local castle and monastery.

The great social and cultural event that the 1902 visit of the sculptor Auguste Rodin certainly was, ended on Sunday June 1. After an official good-bye, the French sculptor, accompanied by Zdenka Brauner and Stanislav Sucharda, went to Moravské Slovácko, at the invitation of a painter and graphic artist Joža Úprk. Rodin also visited the abyss Macocha. He was enthusiastic about the beauty of the Moravian landscape and especially the areas magnificent national costumes. But this was another story... Let us return to Prague, where Rodin's exhibition was extended until August 10, 1902, but despite that ended with a deficit. At the recommendation of the representatives of Bohemian art associations, the City Council purchased Rodin's statue *The Age of Bronze*. The pavilion, originally meant as a temporary structure, resisted pressure from the City Council and the aldermen of Smíchov, to have it demolished, until 1914. Until then, the *Mánes Association* organized its exhibitions in it.

Upon his return to Paris, August Rodin sent a letter, dated June 25, 1902, to the Mayor of Prague, JUDr. Karel Groš, thanking him for his hospitality. The letter was translated into Czech and published on July 16 of the same year in *Národní listy*. The text of the letter was: "Dear Sir, Mayor of Prague, having returned from my visit in Prague, where I was welcomed as an honorable citizen of France and an artist and sculptor, I now have the very pleasant obligation to thank you and your city for your hospitality. Prague is one of the most divine cities. While I was there, my mind often wandered to Rome, which, I believe, resembles Prague more than any other city. You, Sir, Mayor of Prague, as well as your aldermen, have done very much for my exhibition and its organization. The Mánes Association impressed me with its generous devotion and did everything to bring our common goals to completion. During the cordial welcome at the City Hall, I was honored to be sitting next to a great citizen (i.e., the Mayor of Prague). Your deputies, Frič and Neubert, welcomed me, but my tongue was unable to express the feeling of pleasure that you all were giving me. I especially want to express my admiration for your energy and strength which was evident all around me. My humble person was elated for several days by all that cordial reception and I shall never erase the memory of it from my mind. I must not omit to mention the beauty of the celebration, the blooming orchards, the aristocratic beauty of the women, their gracious movements and robes, so charming and elegant as to remind me of Dante's Paradise. I have not yet been able to get the article in *Pražské Listy* translated. In conclusion, let me say that I am happy that my statue The Age of Bronze shall have the honor to be placed in the large conference hall of the City Hall. Affectionately yours, Auguste Rodin."

The famous French sculptor, Auguste Rodin, died on November 17, 1917, in Meudon. In Paris, not far from *Hotel des Invalides*, is a villa which Rodin had bought and where he had his studio - it is Rodin's Museum today. On the anniversary of his death in 1922, a large exhibition was organized in Prague in three locations at once: the St. Anežka Česká Convent at Na Františku, in the Rudolfinum, and in the City Hall of Old Town Prague.

Casp. Pluth: Prague - Vyšehrad, about 1800, colored engraving, detail (Prague - L. Sachs)

Albert

SCHWEITZER

F ew people - in the whole existence of mankind - have given their lives so much sense and fulfillment as the Protestant theologian, philosopher, physician, writer, musicologist, organ player, and above all great philanthropist-humanist Albert Schweitzer. The city of Prague can certainly consider it an honor to have twice hosted this historically great man, in 1923 and again 1928.

Albert Schweitzer was born on January 14, 1875, in Kaysersberg in Upper Alsace, as the second child of an Evangelical parish administrator, Ludwig Schweitzer, and his wife Adela, born Schillinger. Upon graduating from high school in Mühlhausen, he enrolled at Strasbourg University. His exceptionally broad range of interests is evident from his choice of courses, as he simultaneously took theology, philosophy, and natural sciences. Even this was not enough to satisfy his hunger for knowledge. He also enrolled in the music conservatory, where he devoted much time to his life's passion - playing the organ.

An excellent student in all the subjects he took, he began to teach at the Strasbourg University while still a student himself. He became a successful highly-educated, well-rounded young man, who - as the saying goes - had the world spread at his feet and a brilliant career as a scientist, or perhaps musician, before him. But Schweitzer felt a certain inner discontent - he felt something unfulfilled within him. While celebrating his 30th birthday, he made up his mind. He would go to black Africa to treat the sick and help the needy. The impulse or incentive for this decision - which absolutely shocked his friends - may well have been a newspaper article written by Father Boegner about the tragic death of a layman missionary, Henri Chapiuse, at a missionary station in Lambaréné on the river Ogové. The article elaborated on the hardships suffered by the missionaries in Africa, compounded by malicious tropical diseases, ended with a plea for help.

But, in order to realize this vision, Schweitzer needed a medical diploma. So, at the age of thirty, the doctor of philosophy, doctor of theology, and university professor, Albert Schweitzer, returned to his studies - to everyone's utter astonishment - to pursue medicine. In December 1911 he completed his schooling when he passed his medical exam in surgery. A year later he married Helen Bresslau, a registered nurse. She became a lifelong supporter and hard-working helper in his humanitarian pursuits. At Easter in 1913, Schweitzer departed by ship, accompanied by his wife and several assistants, for Equatorial Africa. His destination was the missionary station in Lambaréné on the shore of the river Ogové, in what was then the French colony of Gabon. He was to help the missionaries there, but above all to establish a hospital. As paradoxical as it may appear, the Evangelical Mission Society in Paris was not at all in favor of having Schweitzer in their mission. The Society's consent was finally obtained only after Schweitzer promised to act strictly as a medical missionary, not a spiritual one.

It took about fifteen years for the laboriously built structures, made mostly of local materials, to be accredited the status of a hospital. The Schweitzers put all of their financial means, including own savings, into the project. They would frequently pay the costs of the necessary medication and medical instruments out of their own pockets. They cured even the most terrible diseases which their African patients had, such leprosy, malaria, sleeping sickness, etc. The better reputation the Lambaréné hospital got, the more likely certain global humanitarian organizations or even individuals were to help, financially or materially; but even with this aid, there was still not enough, no matter how much they economized.

To ease the ill effects of the deadly African climate on Europeans, Schweitzer would occasionally interrupt his work in Lambaréné and return to Switzerland. Especially after several years of operating the hospital, he could afford to leave for short period of time since - being a wise man - he had duly educated and trained his medical and nursing teams to be independent. Though in Europe, he did not forget his hospital. It could be said that he combined leisure with useful work. In many cities throughout Europe, he lectured on science, made arrangements for copyrights to his books on a variety of subjects, ranging from philosophy to music history, and gave concerts, mostly on the organ. All these endeavors had a single goal: to collect as much money for the Lambaréné hospital as possible. Schweitzer had an original attitude toward money. He liked to say: "None of us have come to this world with anything. Everything we have was acquired during our life on earth and it is therefore our duty to share our wealth with those who have not been so lucky."

And so it happened that this doctor of Lambaréné arrived in Prague, in January 1923, at the invitation of Oskar Kraus, a professor of the Philosophical Faculty of the German University of Prague. He arrived from Nuremberg, through Cheb, on a third-class ticket, as was usual for him - there were no cheaper tickets to be had. The program was agreed upon in advance: lectures, personal meetings, and concerts. The first organ concert took place on January 12, 1923, in St. Michael's Church, a German Evangelical church in Jircháře. He gave another concert at the same church two days later. The repertoire featured mostly Johann Sebastian Bach. A major organ concert was then given at the St. Kliment Church, a Czech Unity of Brethren church. The priest of that church, Dr. František Bednář, who was simultaneously a professor at the Jan Hus Theological Faculty in Prague, took the honored guest around Prague to show him some of the significant parts of the city. In connection with his lectures in Prague, mostly on philosophical and theological themes, Schweitzer was most willing to meet with anyone who had anything to say on the topic at hand. During this Prague visit, the doctor-philanthropist was also received at the Prague Castle by President T.G. Masaryk. Both philosophers and humanists had a long discussion. After finishing his engagement in Prague, Schweitzer also lectured in other Czech towns.

Towards the end of 1928, Schweitzer came to Prague for the second time. The main reason of his visit was to accept an *honoris causa* degree awarded to him by the Philosophical Faculty of the German University of Prague. Apart from this event, he also lectured and gave concerts in various churches in Prague. One of his organ concerts, held on December 8, 1928, took place at the Smetana Hall of Obecní dům [Communal House]. As a special gesture of friendship to his Prague hosts, Schweitzer added Antonín Dvořák's *Biblical Songs* to the program. Organs were Schweitzer's great love. He not only thoroughly studied the theory of organ music, but also researched the construction of this divine music instrument. As part of this research, he also visited various Prague churches to learn about their organs directly in situ, accompanied by Josef Růžička, an organ player from Prague.

In 1952, Prof. Dr. Albert Schweitzer received the Nobel Peace Prize for his lifelong humanist and humanitarian work. The reason for his being selected for this high honor was, without a doubt, his lifelong creed of pacifism and opposition to nuclear armament. This great European Albert Schweitzer, who had bound his life to Africa, reportedly carried out over 42,000 operations and surgical procedures in his hospital in Lambaréné; he continued to operate until the ripe age of 80 and died on September 4, 1965. Pursuant to his wish, he is buried on the shore of the Ogové river, next to his wife Helen. A simple wood cross that he constructed himself before he died has been erected at his gravesite.

In October 1993, a commemorative plaque was ceremoniously unveiled in memoriam of the founder of the Lambaréné hospital, on the facade of St. Michael's Church in Jircháře, in New Town Prague. At the invitation of the Society of the Friends of Africa and other institutions, among the honored guests of the unveiling ceremony Mrs. Rhena Miller-Schweitzer, daughter of the legendary doctor, was present. The text on the plaque is brief:

"ALBERT SCHWEITZER 1875 KAYSERSBERG † 1965 LAMBARÉNÉ - PERFORMED HERE IN 1923 AND 1928."

František Chalupa: Morning Mood in Prague, Květy VI. 1871;
woodcut (Prague - National Museum Library)

Fyodor Ivanovich

SHALYAPIN

O ne of the most famous opera singers of all times was Fyodor Ivanovich Shalyapin, who was born on February 13, 1873, in Kazan. According to his autobiography, his childhood was miserable. The family was very poor, and his father, Ivan, a notorious alcoholic. At first, he worked as a low-position clerk and scribe, drinking only every 20th day of the month, after pay day, later he would drink daily. After returning from the pub, he would yell at all the members of his family, many times he would beat Fyodor's mother, sometimes to unconsciousness.

Young Fyodor Ivanovich was spellbound by singing. He loved it when his mother sang during rare moments of peace and was enthusiastic over the church choir. The Shalyapins' landlord had a daughter who played the piano. That is when the boy heard this instrument for the first time and the sound of it was something divine. Luck had it that one of the tenants organized a lottery for his old piano. The Shalyapins bought a ticket and - to young Fedya's greatest joy - they won the piano.

But no one was allowed to touch the piano so it would not be damaged, and when the money ran out, the piano left the home.

As a young man, Shalyapin pulled his courage together one day and applied for a position of a chorus singer in a certain entertainment company. The result of the interview proves what a paradox life can be. Shalyapin was not accepted, on account of his voice being too weak, but other aspirants were taken. Among them was Alexey Maximovich Peshkov, who later became famous as a writer, under the pen name Maxim Gorki.

Shalyapin would not be discouraged, especially after he got lucky enough to see a "real theater". Someone put in a word or two on his behalf at the theater and he, directly in the opera department, in fact, got a position as an extra. It was even a paid job - five whole kopecks per show. Soon enough he switched theaters, but could not shake his shyness. One day, playing the role of a policeman, he could not give out a sound when the curtain went up, nor was he able to move. The performance ended in a fiasco and the future star of the most prominent global boards of fame was chased away, earning painful kicks in the behind, in addition to insults from the enraged theater director.

But Shalyapin would not give up. His desire to perform in a theater was simply too strong. He gained his first dramatic experience under most meager living conditions with traveling theater groups. Sometimes he would switch this activity for some heavy physical work, because hunger was, in those days, his most faithful companion. Nevertheless, his immense talent took him towards his goal, step by step. At one point, a former member of the Czar's theater in Moscow, the tenor Usatov, took him under his wing. Not only did he teach the talented young man to sing, but he even found him a sponsor. At the age of 20, Shalyapin was offered permanent engagement at the Tiflin State Opera with a salary of 150 rubles. Celebrating much success both with the audiences and professional critics, he waited for the end of the season and then left for Moscow, by train, equipped with letters of recommendation.

But Shalyapin's road to the height of stardom was not nearing its end yet. One of the happy stopovers in his life was an encounter with a very wealthy man and art supporter, as well as connoisseur of music, Sava Ivanovich Mamontov. Enraptured by his voice, Mamontov engaged Shalyapin in his recently founded private theater and opera. Shalyapin career was on its way up.

At the beginning of the new century, he was invited to accept a guest engagement in La Scala in Milan. He sang in Boito's *Mefistofele* and it was a success in every way. He did a concert tour of Europe and, in 1907, he performed on yet another prestigious world stage - the Metropolitan Opera in New York. Shalyapin had very peculiar ideas of the parts he sang and was very demanding with stage designers, but his repertoire was incredibly large. As his fame grew, so did his financial demands for individual performances.

At the beginning of World War I, Shalyapin returned to Russia to perform there, in his native land. But the Bolshevik Revolution in 1917 affected his professional and private life, just like many other people's. Although he had a very strong social conscience, he could not come to terms with the new social order and, in 1921, he left Russia with his whole family. Several years before this, in 1898, he had married an Italian dancer named Tornegi. He then settled permanently in Paris. Although he was been lured and enticed to return, and his homesickness was great, he never went back.

After his departure from Russia, he went on grand-scale tour so that practically the whole world became acquainted with his singing. He traveled to North and South America, Australia, China, Japan, Ceylon (Sri Lanka today), and Singapore. He was in his time considered the best bass opera singer. In addition to much popularity, his tour brought him considerable financial revenues. For several years, he had a permanent engagement with the Metropolitan Opera, New York.

Shalyapin arrived in Prague, one of the traditional centers of European music culture, in 1925. His performance - Borodino's opera *Count Igor* - before a sold-out audience at the National Theater was an enormous success. On October 9, 1925, he also held a solo concert in the grand hall of the *Lucerna* Palace. Although the ticket price was more expensive than usual, for the artist was fully aware of his singularity, there was not an empty seat in the audience. Shalyapin performed the whole range of his repertoire, from Russian folk songs to the most difficult arias from famous operas. His success was enormous. His performance at the *Lucerna* Palace is remembered by Václav M. Havel in his memoirs published in Samizdat in 1977.

During his second visit to Prague, in 1930, Shalyapin performed at the National Theater again, in Boris Godunov, his favorite opera. The orchestra of the Bratislava Opera was conducted by Oskar Nedbal. The artist also gave a separate concert. He was accommodated in New Town Prague, in the, now non-existent, Hotel de Saxe on the corner of Hybernská and Senovážná Streets. The hotel went out of its way for the star; even the room was rearranged exactly according to the artist's wishes.

Despite his globetrotting lifestyle, Fyodor Ivanovich Shalyapin felt like a Slav and was very proud of it. He adored Bohemian music, especially the music of its two leading composers, Bedřich Smetana and Antonín Dvořák. He was also determined to settle in one of the Slavic countries in his old age. The possibility of retiring in his native Russia was up in the air and he was much more inclined to try to purchase some property, probably a small castle, somewhere in Czechoslovakia and settle there. During one of his visits he was even received by the President of the Republic, T. G. Masaryk. In his diary of 1931, the President made a note of having been to a Shalyapin concert.

During one of his subsequent visit, in 1934, Shalyapin sang *Don Quixote* in French in Jules Massenet's opera of the same name, directed by Hanuš Thein. Other leading parts were sung by the following artists: Beautiful Dulcinea by Štěpánka Štěpánková and Sancho by Jan Konstantin. During the rehearsal for this opera, and during the actual performance, Shalyapin conducted himself like a real prima donna. In fact, whole legends are told about his behavior on many other occasions, as well.

For instance, during the rehearsal of *Don Quixote*, Shalyapin wanted to redo the entire set, including a door. Upon hearing a patient explanation that it was not technically possible, he pulled out a knife, cut a hole in the prop, and entered the scene from a spot which suited his particular notions. During the premiere, he refused to sing without a live horse and donkey, strictly demanding that they be on the stage too. With much hassle, these two living creatures had to be procured somewhere in Prague and brought on the stage during Shalyapin's aria. This sequence was severely hampered by the proverbial stubbornness of the little donkey which simply refused to cross the stage and no method of coercion could convince it to do so. The audience broke out in laughter and the earnestness of the performance was seriously affected. After the first act of the opera, Shalyapin demanded to be paid right away - in contradiction to the agreement which set the day of payment for the next day - refusing to continue until his pay was delivered. As was mentioned before, his financial demands were quite steep, so the cash was not on hand. He decided he would wait until all the money was put together and delivered, ' and only then would he finish his part. In the final act of the opera, where the "dejected knight" dies, Shalyapin suddenly interrupted his solo part, went to the edge of the stage to scold the conductor in the orchestra underneath the stage for playing the aria at a wrong rhythm, returned to his scene and finished dying. No one but the ingenious Shalyapin could have got away with such nonsense, but he did.

Fyodor Ivanovich Shalyapin performed in Prague for the last time in 1937. The next year, on April 12, 1938, he died in Paris. He is buried at the famous Parisian cemetery Père Lachaise.

Vincenc Morstadt: Old Town Tower with Charles Bridge, 1842,
watercolor (Prague - National Museum)

Alexander Vasilyevich

SUVOROV

During the Napoleonic Wars, Prague was frequently a throughway for smaller or even larger military formations. For the Old Town population, it was a welcome show to see military heroes, so to speak, with their own eyes. In addition, it was a chance for them to learn some news about situation at the front. If the soldiers stayed in Prague or its vicinity, evenings in the pubs would be brimming with embellished combat stories, in which the narrator was, more often than not, illustrated as the hero. Pragonians quickly realized that the truth of the triumphs or defeats could more easily be told by the number of horses returning with emply saddles.

This is how, on December 20, 1799, the famous Russian commander, Generalissimo Alexander Vasilyevich Suvorov (1730 - 1800), arrived in Prague with his staff and a part of his regiment. Pragonians were very excited over the prospect of seeing the distinguished guest who had run Napoleon and his army out of Northern Italy. Suvorov, who had his son with him, moved into a large palace-like building, No. 37, whose front wall faced the New Alley, Národní třída today.

The house belonged to a Prague native, Jakub Wimmer (1754 - 1822). The host himself had had a fairly extensive military career and had also demonstrated extraordinary organizational skills during the transport of building material to a military fortress named Terezín. He had been authorized not only to manage the entire transportation system in the Austrian Army, but also to restructure its engineering system. For his merits, he was promoted to the rank of colonel and awarded the Order of St. Stephen, in addition to being given nobility and receiving the title of a baron.

The fact that Suvorov was accommodated in Wimmer's house clearly proves the clout which Jakub Wimmer must have had at the Imperial court in Vienna. The Court's wish was to continue to cooperate with the Russian Czar, so the order was made to devote the best possible care to Suvorov. An honor guard comprising of a flag-bearer, trumpeter, and drummer would stand round the clock at the entrance to the house. Whenever the Generalissimo would come and go from his temporary quarters, the New Alley would resonate with ceremonial fanfare, attracting the attention of everyone within earshot.

A culturally rich program was prepared for Suvorov consisting of banquets, balls, and concerts. On December 22, 1799, Stavovské Theater performed the opera Count Tarentský. It seemed that the ovations which the enthusiastic audience gave the celebrated military hero would never and. The audience even chanted: "Long live Hero Suvorov!" It is said that the war-hardened veteran shed tears on receiving such a welcome.

On a different note, Suvorov reportedly - according to the diary of a well-known physician and head physician at the Charity Brethren Hospital at Na Františku, Jan Theobald Held (1770 - 1851) - committed a minor social faux-pas. During a walk in town, in Husova St. near the Dominican Monastery of St. Aegidius, he met a brewer called Spirit from the Perštýn Brewery. Suvorov, on seeing his dark clothing, mistook the man for a priest and before his companion could stop him, he rushed to kiss his hand. The brewer was stunned speechless, but eventually, stuttering, tried to explain who he was.

According to the doctor's description, his stuttering was so inarticulate and incoherent that today's listener might think the man was emitting messages in Morse code.

In a formerly famous hotel on Malá Strana, called *V Lázních* [In the Baths], a magnificent ball was organized on January 19, 1800, in Suvorov's honor, simultaneously with a banquet honoring his countryman, the Count Peter Ivanovich Bagration, a Russian general. In the front part of the grand salon, the organizers hung a huge billboard depicting all the battles in which Generalissimo Suvorov had actively fought. Across from the painted board stood a decorated sofa where Suvorov was strategically seated so as to have good view of the dancing couples as well as the battle scenes on the board. He was also told that the painting - the work of Josef Březina (1758-1818), who also painted the interior of Stavovské Theater in Prague - was a gift for him. Considering the size of that creation, it was a truly Danaian gift. But Suvorov was not only an excellent strategist, but also a diplomat. He gave thanks for the painting and, after some thought, gave it to the owner of the establishment, Jan Tichý, who was overjoyed by this generosity. He also assured the Generalissimo that he would have the battle scenes properly lit on the very next festive occasion.

Another major ceremony in honor of Suvorov was held on January 25, 1800, at the hotel *U Zlatého jednorožce* [Golden Unicorn], house No. 285, at Lázeňská 11, on Malá Strana, which had already become famous in the past when the music composer Ludwig van Beethoven stayed there. This time, the festive event attended by select members of high society in honor of the seventy-year-old Generalissimo was organized by Michael Miloradovich, a Russian general. The tables were heavily laden with delectable food and drink. For the pleasure of the guests' noble ears, there were two orchestras, playing alternately, on a stage covered with fabrics in Russian and Austrian national colors.

The imperial court in Vienna expressed a wish to have a portrait of Suvorov. The Viennese court painter, named Schmidt, was sent to Prague for that purpose. But due to all his many social engagements, the veteran soldier showed consideration for the court painter's task only when sitting at lunch. This caused no technical problem for the painter, but one of another type, for Suvorov was always dressed in a Russian peasant shirt - *rubashka*. He turned a deaf ear to the painter's pleas to don his festive uniform. Schmidt was therefore forced to work without it and add it to the portrait subsequently. Color prints of Generalissimo Suvorov, accompanied by some biographical data, were sold around Bohemia, also in the *Česká expedice* store of publisher Václav Matěj Kramerius.

Today, house No. 37 on Národní třída bears a bilingual plaque featuring also the bust of the Generalissimo. The text announces that the Generalissimo of the Russian Army, Alexander Vasilyevich Suvorov, lived there from December 20, 1799, to January 28, 1800.

Upon leaving Prague, Suvorov, who had in the course of his military career contributed a great deal to Russian military education and made history with his modern approach to combat techniques and also by his invincibility, went back to Russia. In May of the same year he died there.

Job Wechter after Filip van den Bossche: Prague, The Stone
(Charles) Bridge and Old Town Prague, 1606, engraving, detail
from a lithograph published by V. Poláček in 1945

AVIA FLVVIVS

175

Peter Ilich

ᎢCHAIKOVSKY

T he best known Russian music composer, Peter Ilich
Tchaikovsky (1840 - 1893) visited Prague three times
in all: twice in 1888 and then again in 1892. The
incentive for his first visit was an invitation of the Music
Department of Umělecká Beseda (Arts Society) in Prague.
Tchaikovsky traveled by train from Dresden and - as was
common in those days - a welcoming delegation was sent to
Kralupy nad Vltavou, where the first part of the official welcome
took place. Upon arrival at Prague, the honorable guest was
received with such honors as are reserved only for the heads of
states. Hybernská Railway Station (Masaryk Station today),
where the train arrived was literally packed with people.
Welcoming speeches were frequently interrupted with
exclamations, like *Nazdar* [hurray], and there were the usual
costumed representatives of all the civil associations. Despite
overwhelming excitement, the organizers of the event managed
to keep the ceremonious reception within reasonable limits, so
that the ever-present Austrian Police, prepared to take strict

measures against explicit signs of Russophilia or Panslavism, found no opportunity to intervene. Tchaikovsky, who was accompanied on that trip to Prague by Alexander Siloti, a Russian piano virtuoso, was staying in a hotel *U Saského dvora* (Saxony Court), one of the most prominent Prague hotels, which used to be located in house No. 997 on the corner of Hybernská and Senovážná Streets.

Peter Ilich Tchaikovsky was born on May 7, 1840, in Votkinsk on the shore of the river Kama, where his father, Ilja Petrovich, was working as a mining engineer. The famous composer's brother, Modest Ilich Tchaikovsky was a well-known playwright and author of a three-volume biography of Peter Ilich. According to numerous literary, periodical, and newspaper sources, the Tchaikovsky family was totally indifferent to music and the sole person who understood and supported young Peter Ilich' interest in music was his French governess Fanny Dürbach. Already at a very early age, he was proficient in French and German; he started to take piano lessons at the age of five years.

When Peter reached adolescence, his father took him to St. Petersburg to enroll him in a college-level law school. Succumbing to his son's enthusiasm for music, he agreed to take him to an experienced piano teacher, Master Kündinger, who however, upon listening to his playing, was very skeptical: "Nothing exceptional - we've got able youngsters like this enough to make a river dam of them." This harsh statement determined the future of Tchaikovsky as a musician, as far as the family was concerned, and thus he entered his law studies.

Although he finished the school and began to work as a civil servant at the ministry of justice, his interest in music won out after all. He enrolled himself in music lessons, which he took after work, and later registered in the St. Petersburg Music Conservatory. The Conservatory was at that time directed by Anton Grigorievich Rubinstein, one of the greatest pianists of the second half of the last century. He completed his studies at the Conservatory in 1865, with a silver award of honor. But the cantata, which he composed as a dissertation work for his diploma and which was performed at the graduation concert, was a total flop with the critics.

Tchaikovsky left St. Petersburg for Moscow to teach music. At first he lectured music theory at a school founded by the

Russian Music Society and then he taught harmony at a newly-opened music conservatory. He stayed at the conservatory, which was run by the brother of Anton Grigorievich Rubinstein. Nikolai, for 12 long years. During the time in Moscow, he began to compose music systematically, but his works were received with mixed success. A turning point in his life came in the person of Nadezhda von Meck, a railroad magnate's widow who became his overwhelmingly generous patroness. An interesting detail in the matter is that, despite frequent exchange of correspondence, they never met personally. Her sponsorship allowed Tchaikovsky to abandon his pedagogical activities, which deprived him of much of his energy, and enabled him to devote all his time to music composition.

In 1877, all of a sudden and to a great surprise of his friends and acquaintances, Tchaikovsky married Antonia Miliukova, whom he had met some time ago. Although he had warned her that he could only be her friend - and she agreed - Tchaikovsky could not cope with the situation psychologically and, barely two weeks into the marriage, he literally fled from it. Under much stress, he even made a passive attempt at suicide - for the first time. He stood, on purpose, for two hours up to his waistline in the cold water of the Moscow river, never finding courage enough to drown himself. Thanks to his youth, the sole consequence of this unsuccessful attempt was a cold.

To escape his own brooding and pull himself together, he departed for a trip around Europe. During his travels, he composed symphonies and developed a fascination for opera. He composed ten of them in all. Of his operas, it was *Eugene Onegin*, above all, that was to achieve world fame. Its premiere took place in 1879 in Moscow and was described by the author himself as a sequence of lyrical scenes. Another of his operas, *The Queen of Spades*, was written during Tchaikovsky's stay in Florence in 1890.

In 1888, Tchaikovsky - as was mentioned above - arrived to Prague for the first time as a guest of the Music Department of Umělecká Beseda. Beseda's aim was to improve the artistic standard of its Popular Concerts Program, for, without any doubt, a prominent personality like Tchaikovsky could certainly help Beseda upgrade the musical scene. On the day of Tchaikovsky's arrival, on February 12, the National Theater gave a festive performance of Verdi's opera *Othello*, which the

Maestro heard for the first time. After the first act, Tchaikovsky was introduced to František Ladislav Rieger and Antonín Dvořák, the leading representatives of Prague's political and musical scene, respectively. After the performance, a reception banquet was held at the hotel *U Saského dvora* [Saxony Court].

The following two days were planned for a tour around Prague. The first day ended with a festive ball held at the large restaurant hall on Žofín Island, the second day was concluded with a festive concert of Bohemian chamber music, organized by Umělecká Beseda. Tchaikovsky was enthusiastic over the Prague Castle, St. Vitus Cathedral, and the magnificent views of Prague. Wherever he went, he was received most attentively - everyone wanted to be near him and shake his hand. A shy man by nature, Tchaikovsky was very uneasy when faced with so much attention. One of the dinners in his honor was prepared for him at the house of Antonín Dvořák, at Žitná Street, No. 564/14. He found the menus so much to his liking that he made a note of it, praising Mrs. Dvořák's cooking skills, in his diary. Today, the house on Žitná Street bears a commemorative plaque inscribed with Tchaikovsky's relief portrait. Unveiled on May 22, 1984, the plaque was created in the workshop of Štefan Malatinec.

The concert of Peter Ilich Tchaikovsky, which was to be held on Sunday, February 19, 1888, at the Rudolfinum in Prague, was anticipated with very high expectations. Preparations for the concert were scrutinized and presented in the press so frequently, that it was finally decided that the rehearsals be made accessible to the public. The first rehearsal of the works programmed for an orchestral concert was held on February 15, 1888, conducted by Tchaikovsky himself. The Master was content with the music skills of both the members of the National Theater orchestra and the guest instrumentalists recruited from the staff of the Prague Music Conservatory. Performed before a packed audience, the concert as such was an extraordinary success. As was common on such special occasions, a large banquet was held after the concert at the hotel *U Saského dvora*, attended by many prominent guests, including the mayor of Prague, JUDr. Jindřich Šolc. Among the guests was also the music composer Antonín Dvořák, who was to become a close longtime friend to Tchaikovsky. Tchaikovsky was sincerely sorry not to have had a chance to see the performance of Dvořák's opera, *Dimitri*. At the banquet, Tchaikovsky held a speech, which he had translated into Czech and also read in that language. The Master mentions this day in his diary as the happiest day in his life.

Another concert, at the National Theater, this time, was planned for February 21, 1888. Again, the public was thrilled and the performance climaxed not once but twice as Tchaikovsky's *String Symphony* and then the second act of his *Swan Lake* was played. Again, a festive banquet followed the concert at the hotel *U Saského dvora*, again. This day, too, Tchaikovsky described in his diary as "minutes of absolute bliss."

During his first visit to Prague, Tchaikovsky managed to see and do an incredible variety of things, with the aid of his guide and interpreter, A. O. Pater, the librarian of the National Museum. He also viewed the collections of the National Museum which were at that time on display in the Nostitz Palace at Na Příkopě. Of the other points of interest, he visited the music inn *U Medvídků* [Little Bear Inn] at Na Perštýně, Náprstek's Ladies' American Club located in the house *U Halánků* [Halanek's House] on Betlémské náměstí [Bethlehem Square] and, of course, also Mozart's *Bertramka* [Bertram's Villa] in Smíchov. At the St. Nicholas Russian Orthodox Church in Old Town Prague, he attended concerts where his own music compositions were played. He was very pleased when members of the Hlahol Choir came in the evening to hotel, holding burning torches in their hands, to sing him a good-night serenade. The Maestro promised he would compose a festive composition for their choir.

Tchaikovsky made a number of friendships in Prague. In addition to Antonín Dvořák, he befriended Zdeněk Fibich, Jan Strakatý, Otakar Hostinský, Betty Fibich, an opera singer, and Maria Červinka-Rieger, a librettist, writer, and translator of the libretto to Tchaikovsky's opera *Eugene Onegin* into Czech. All these personalities and many others came to see Tchaikovsky off as he was leaving Prague for Paris and London to tend to his concert commitments.

In the same year, on November 27, 1888, Tchaikovsky visited Prague again to give a grand concert at the National Theater. The highlight of this visit to Prague was the Prague premiere of *Eugene Onegin* which Tchaikovsky himself conducted. The performance was an absolute triumph for him. The role of Eugene Onegin was sung by Bohumil Benoni and the role of Tatiana by Berta Foerster-Lauterer. The Composer was radiant and declared that the performance of the leading female role, in particular, was absolutely perfect.

The third time that Tchaikovsky visited Prague was on October 8, 1892. Like on both previous occasions, this time, too, he stayed at the hotel *U Saského dvora*. On October 11, 1892, the National Theater, sold out to the last seat, was witness to the Prague premiere of another Tchaikovsky's opera, *The Queen of Spades*. The performance was a huge success and the composer, very happy and generally content, left Prague the following day, promising to return soon again. Little did he anticipate that fate would not let him fulfill that promise.

Psychologically a rather unstable man, Tchaikovsky composed yet another of his supreme compositions during what was to be his last creative period: *The Sixth Symphony*, known as *Symphonie Pathétic*. On November 6, 1893, he died in St. Petersburg. The cause of his death has not been fully clarified to this day. Official medical records state the cause of his death to be cholera, which he reportedly contracted upon drinking a glass of unboiled water. It is also believed that his brother, Modest, who was of the same sexual orientation, may have had a share of guilt in his death, as it is known that the two brothers had had a fight over one and the same lover. Another version claims that he had been driven to suicide (by arsenic) by the Court of Honor, when his relationship to a certain young man, whose father was very influential at the Czar's court, was exposed..

Although Peter Ilich Tchaikovsky will never physically visit Prague again, his music will be present forever. Just to mention a few examples: in 1994, the National Theater held a premiere of *Eugene Onegin* and on May 17, 1998, the premiere of *The Queen of Spades*.

Vincenc Morstadt, View of the Old Town Tower with Charles
Bridge, sideways in the background are seen the buildings of
the Knights of the Cross Monastery, sepia-watercolor drawing,
1824 (Prague - National Museum)

Carl Maria von

WEBER

T he Holstein native, Carl Maria von Weber, author of the ingenious *Der Freischütz*, engraved his name in the music history of Prague through his engagement with the Prague Opera, where he was conductor from 1813 to 1816. Although preliminary arrangements in that respect had already been made, it turned out that von Weber had been planning a concert tour of Italy and he had to be persuaded to alter his plans. After the retirement of the current head of the Opera, Václav Müller, it was necessary to replace him with an distinguished personality in music. The aristocratic patrons of the Stavovské Theater, Count Isidor of Lobkowitz, supreme Markrave Kolovrat-Liebstein, and Count Christian Clam-Gallas took it upon themselves to resolve the problem. When the coercion was joined even by the director of the Theater, Karel Liebich, Weber finally gave his consent. His decision was undoubtedly facilitated by a solid financial offer and a guarantee of two to three months' vacation. Upon signing his contract, Weber became not only the orchestra master but also the director of the opera department of Stavovské Theater.

The future founder and creator of the German romantic opera as a genre, Carl Maria von Weber, was born on December 18, 1786, in Utting in Holstein. It is more than likely that no blue blood circulated in his veins. The aristocratic particle "von" must have been adopted by his worldly father, Franz Anton, who took example from other nouveau-rich of the time. Young Carl Maria divided his time between music and painting, but music eventually took precedence, and thanks to his father's understanding, he soon received musical training. He studied piano, voice, and composition. He wrote the first of his major compositions, an opera titled *The Dryad*, as early as 1800. It was played even in Prague, in the Czech language. After making his debut in the Vienna music world, he got an engagement as a director of the opera in Wroclaw, where he formed a new orchestra and chorus, composed, and gave concerts.

By the time Weber arrived in Prague, he already was an accomplished composer, conductor, and concert master of high repute. It is certain that, by engaging him in Prague, an important step was taken towards the restoration of the Czech opera scene. Weber produced several dozen plays at the Stavovské Theater. In fact, his very first performance was related to an opera which came to be associated with Prague and Stavovské Theater through a touch of destiny: Mozart's *Don Giovanni*. In staging the piece, Weber was so uncompromising that - as a gesture of spite to director Liebich's cost-cutting measures - he paid the musicians out of his own pocket just to have them on the stage during the ball scene.

During his stay in Prague, Weber lived in Old Town Prague in house No. 450, known as *Vratislavský dům*, at 16 Jilská Street. He lived within a few minutes' walking distance from Stavovské Theater.

Weber wrote enthusiastic letters to his friends about a concert which he had attended in Prague on March 6, 1813, at the Reduta Hall. Among other musical works, he played his own compositions, entitled *Concert, Hymnus*, and *Symphony*. The vocals were sung by Anna Müller. Critics' reviews were mostly positive, but it was not possible to please everyone. For instance, Weber was reproached for preferring his own compositions and for performing music that was too mystical at times. But Weber hardly took little of the criticism to heart, nor was he aware that changes in the opera orchestra continued to gradually adapt to his own ideas. On the other hand, thanks to his undeniable influence in the artistic world, he managed to draw new musicians and soloists to the Stavovské Theater stage. One of his fist such accomplishments was the hiring of Karolina Brandt.

The year 1813 was wartime. Refugees poured into Prague from Saxony and Prussia. Weber proved his strong social compassion when he organized a charity concert on September 14, with the proceeds of 810 guilders donated to their benefit. He organized a similar event some time later, this time to the benefit of a Prague poorhouse, and another charity concert to the benefit of widows and orphans of musicians. It is important to note that he produced these benefit concerts while being virtually inundated with work, as he was in charge of both the artistic and organizational aspects of each performance.

During the first year of his career in Prague, Weber fell very deeply in love. As a man, he could not be indifferent to the renowned beauty of Terezia Frey. The primary obstacle in the matter was that the object of his affection was already married to the master of choreography, Brunetti, with whom she had a twelve-year-old daughter. Weber secretly gave the daughter lessons in piano and voice. It had to be in secret, because when the time was right, he wanted to surprise his beloved Terezia Frey with her daughter's progress. Terezia kept her heart open to other suitors as well, causing Weber many moments of suffering. He confided in his diary, in which he wrote regularly, confessing that he was hurt so deeply that he was sometimes brought to tears.

Fortunately for Weber, the scene was entered by the entrance of Karolina Brandt, the no less beautiful but much younger daughter of a concert master and tenor, Luis Brandt. As mentioned above, she was a soloist of the Prague Opera. On January 1, 1814, she had her enormously successful debut in the role of Cinderella, but she also performed in dramatic plays. The two young people felt a mutual attraction which led to their engagement - although Weber was turned down on the first try - and then marriage.

Despite his heavy work schedule, Carl Maria Weber led a very active social, public, and above all cultural life. He found time to attend gatherings with friends, which were held at a house in Libeň, or rather an estate, called *Na ztracené vartě* [Lost Sentry Post] owned by the director of Stavovské Theater, Karel Liebich. He invited his friends and colleagues frequently - in fact, that is where Weber got a chance to approach Karolina Brandt.

But everything has its end and so did Weber's artistic engagement in Prague. At Easter in 1816, Weber withdrew from his contract with Stavovské Theater and the Prague Opera. Proof of his personal integrity lays in the fact that he had the following announcement printed, at his expense, in the press: "Appeal! My future artistic plans force me to give up my directorship of the Prague Opera as of the end of September 1818. As I am most sincerely interested in seeing this meticulously directed institution passed into good hands, I have the honor to appeal - with the consent from the honorable Directorate of the Theater - to artists who might be interested in the position to kindly contact the entrepreneur and director of the Royal Bohemian Stavovské Theater, Mr. Karel Liebich, or myself." The appeal was dated May 24, 1816, in Prague, signed by C. M. v. Weber, former Opera Director and Orchestra Master of the Royal Bohemian Stavovské Theater in Prague. Another of his announcements was published in this manner as a good-bye to his colleagues. The second announcement hinted tactfully at the reasons for his decision. It was printed on October 4, 1916. Three days thereafter, Weber and Karolina Brandt left Prague in a coach headed for Berlin.

This, however, was not the only loss which befell Stavovské Theater. On December 21, in the same year, the popular long-time director of the Theater, Karel Liebich, died from an extended illness. He was interred two days later in the presence of a large crowd of people. The management of the Theater was taken over by his widow, Johanna Liebich.

Carl Maria von Weber returned to Prague the very next year. The reason for his return was very important and pleasant, too: on November 4, 1817, he married the love of his life, the blond-haired Karolina Brandt, at the St. Jindřich Church in New Town Prague. Before the wedding, the couple went to confession and took communion. The wedding was conducted by Father de Bery; the witnesses were Dr. Jungh, a physician, and Ignatius Kleinwächter, a banker. The bride got a piece of golden jewelry and a shawl from the groom as a wedding present. The wedding feast was held at the house of one of the witnesses. The day thereafter, the newlyweds went on their honeymoon.

In May 1821, the premiere of Weber's opera *Der Freischütz* was performed in Berlin. It was an enormous success and became Weber's best-known masterpiece. The opera was also known under other working titles, such as Enchanted Bullets, A Trial Shot, The Hunter's Bride, etc., but ultimately it was to be *Der Freischütz*. On February 13, 1822, Weber came to Prague once again, this time terminally ill, to personally and successfully conduct the performance of the *Der Freischütz*.

Carl Maria von Weber, an artist whose name is written in the world history of music in bold letters, died in London of a throat tuberculosis in the small hours of the night on June 5, 1826. He would have turned forty years old that year. Shortly before his death, he attended several very successful performances of his last opera, Oberon. He was buried to the sounds of Mozart's Requiem in the crypt of St. Mary's Church in Noorfield, from where his bodily remains were transported to Dresden in December 1844.

Jan Josef Dietzler: The Cattle Market (Charles Square) with
New Town Municipal Hall, during the coronation parade in
honor of Maria Teresia. Appendix to *Drey Beschreibungen* by
J. H. Ramhoff, Prague 1743. Engraving by J. A. Pfeffel, Augsburg
(Prague - National Museum)

Elizabeth Johanna
(Westonia)

WESTON

A prominent English Renaissance poetess who lived at the break of the 16th and 17th centuries, Elizabeth Johanna Weston (1582 - 1612), known also as Westonia, arrived in Prague with her parents, John and Johanna, and her older brother Frank, after the family was expelled from their homeland. At that time, England was ruled by Queen Elizabeth, and the country was boiling over with religious and political discontent. While crossing the Channel, the sea was stormy and huge waves badly damaged the boat. The Westons were lucky to have survived. Upon landing in Holland, they realized very soon what it meant to be refugees. No longer welcome at home, unwelcome abroad, and dependent on people's mercy. Their journey across France and Italy to Bohemia was full of woe, strewn with adversity and obstacles.

The Weston family settled first in Český Krumlov, then in Rožmberk, on the estate of powerful gentry - the Rožmberks. The father, John, himself of noble descent, succeeded in getting an audience with Peter Vok of Rožmberk (1539 - 1611). According to eye witnesses, he fell to his knees, telling the aristocrat of his family's terrible fate and begging him for help. Peter Vok, one of the most powerful and wealthiest men in the Bohemian Kingdom, had sympathy for the family's plight and provided them with financial support. He also spoke to Emperor Rudolf II, so the Westons traveled first to Prague and a few days later moved North, to Most, where they were taken to a house to live in.

John Weston, wishing for wealth and a return to high society, was easily diverted from the path of common sense and turned to alchemy. Like others in those days, he performed many experiments. It was during one of these, as he was heating up some unknown amalgam, that the substance exploded and he was seriously injured. He died a few days later. Thus the family lost its sole provider, albeit occasional, and found itself on the verge of utter poverty once again. John Weston was buried in Most and his son Frank departed, as was planned before his father's death, to study in Ingolstadt, where he died in 1600, without ever seeing his mother or sister again. The two women left Most for Prague, hoping to improve the state of their finances.

Once in Prague, they tried to get an audience with the Emperor again, but this time did not succeed. Johanna Weston met one of her famous - or rather infamous, as it turned out later - countrymen in Prague, the alchemist Kelley, and married him. Edward Kelley was at that time still enjoying the Emperor's confidence and favors. He was, therefore, well off, both socially and financially. The desperate plight of mother and daughter was for the time being averted. They both moved into house No. 502 and 503 at Karlovo náměstí, generally known as *Faustův dům* [Faust's house] today, in New Town Prague. Elizabeth Johanna Weston was not only exceptionally beautiful, but also had a literary talent; as Kelley's stepdaughter, she could begin her education, systematically, and develop her gift for poetry.

The material security did not last long. Kelley killed another of the Emperor's favorites in a duel, and the Emperor added this crime to the list of empty promises of instant gold. The Emperor had him imprisoned at the Křivoklát castle. Moreover, he had all Kelley's property, i.e., real estate and chattels, confiscated. Johanna Weston pleaded with the Emperor to change his mind, but in vain. In 1597, Edward Kelley, Elizabeth Johanna Weston's stepfather, died in prison.

Back to poverty, once again, Elizabeth continued in her studies diligently. She knew English, French, Italian, German, Czech, and Latin. It was in Latin that she also wrote her poetry. The women were finally saved from ruin by Jindřich of Písnice, the Imperial scrivener, who took both women into his house and even supported Elizabeth's brother in Ingolstadt. The young poetess took up a long and exhausting battle for the restitution of her stepfather's property. In versed petitions she would try to cajole even Emperor Rudolf II. Let us add that all her efforts were in vain. In 1602, Weston got only marginal indemnification in the amount of 1,000 thalers - a ridiculous amount, compared to the worth of the confiscated property.

She was saved from her situation by marriage, like her mother years before. In 1603, Elizabeth Johanna Weston was married in St. Thomas Church in Malá Strana. Her husband was John Leo of Isenac, ambassador and councilman to His Highness, the Archduke of Bavaria, Nassau, Lüneburg, and Count of Anhalt at the Imperial Court. The wedding was a return to higher society, for she was completely penniless at that time. Now she finally could devote time to poetry, in addition to her marital and motherly duties. She had, of course, plenty of both. During the last nine years of her life, she gave birth to seven children. Three of them died shortly after birth and only four sons survived their mother.

The collected poems of Elizabeth Johanna Weston were published the first time in 1602 in Frankfurt an der Oder, then in 1606 in Prague, in 1609 in Leipzig, and in 1723, post mortem, in Frankfurt am Main. The poems depict her uneasy, and even adventurous life, to a certain extent. A book of her poems is deposited at the National Library in Rudolfinum. Some of them have been translated into Czech by František Ladislav Čelakovský (1799 - 1852). During the Renaissance, her work was famous around the world. She was called the tenth Muse, fourth Grace, female Ovidius, or world's miracle. In 1601, Paul Melisseus, a French aristocrat, poet and Weston's contemporary, who lived at the court of Emperor Rudolf II, sent her a laurel wreath and an Ode dedicated to her.

The poetess Elizabeth Johanna Weston died at the age of only thirty years, on November 23, 1612, in Prague. She was buried in the same church, St. Thomas's Church in Malá Strana, where she had been wed just nine years before. The church - as was usual in Rudolfinian Prague - was built with a courtyard in which prominent persons would be buried. Of the other personages buried there, let us mention Oldřich Avostalis (+ 1597), a builder, Adrian de Vries (+ 1626), sculptor and metal-caster. Elizabeth Johanna Weston's husband, John Leo of Isenac, commissioned a tombstone for her carved with a lion and right crosses. The epitaph engraved in it was written by the above mentioned Paul Melisseus. The Czech translation of the Latin inscription says: "To Elizabeth Johanna Weston, whose celebrated homeland was dignified England, to the Sulpitia of our ages, whose knowledge is a fresh flower to Minerva, an adornment to Suade, a pleasure to Muse, and a model to women." The tombstone can be seen by today's visitors at the renovated Augustinian monastery, near the entrance of the monastery gate. It is built into the southern wall of the monastery, occupying the last space in the line, from the perspective of an in-coming visitor.

Selected bibliography:

Cenek Edvard: T. A. Edison
Prague 1947.

Čeleda Jaroslav: Paganini a Praha (Paganini and Prague)
Prague 1940.

Farga Franz: Paganini.
Prague 1969.

Hádek Karel: Čtení o staré Praze (Readings of Old Prague)
Prague 1940.

Herain Jan: Karlův most v Praze (Charles Bridge in Prague)
Prague 1908.

Herain Jan - Matiegka Jindřich: Tycho Brahe.
Časopis přátel starožitností českých v Praze - Prague 1901.
(Magazine of the Friends of Bohemian Antiques)

Hippmann Silvestr: Fryderyk Chopin.
Prague 1946.

Hlobil I. - Chotěbor P. - Mahler Z.: Katedrála sv. Víta I (St. Vitus Cathedral I)
Prague 1994.

Horský Zdeněk: Kepler v Praze (Kepler in Prague)
Prague 1980.

Hrubeš Josef - Hrubešová Eva: Pražské domy vyprávějí III
(Prague Houses Tell Stories III)
Prague 1997.

Kopylov D.: F. I. Šaljapin.
Prague 1947.

Korbelová Helena: Rodinova pražská výstava a jeho návštěva v Praze.
(Rodin's Exhibition and Visit in Prague)
Documenta Pragensia č. 2 - Prague 1981.

Kuna Milan: Čajkovskij a Praha (Tchaikovsky and Prague)
Prague 1980.

Marek Jan: Auguste Rodin.
Přemožitelé času č. 3 - Prague 1987.

Němec Zdeněk: Weberova pražská léta (Weber's Years in Prague)
Prague 1944.

Plevka Bohumil: Petr Iljič Čajkovskij.
Přemožitelé času č. 2 - Prague 1987.

Soukup J. B.: Enrico Caruso.
Prague 1949.

Šaljapin Fedor I.: Z mého života (Stories from my Life)
Rumburk 1946.

Toulky hudební Prahou - autor neuveden. (Wandering Round Musical
Prague)
Prague 1949.

Wenig Jan: Byli v Praze. (They have been to Prague.)
Prague 1970.

Contents

FOREIGNERS IN PRAGUE

Text: JOSEF HRUBEŠ and EVA HRUBEŠOVÁ

Translation into Englisch:
MIRA TRANSLATION
Vladimíra Ráftlová M. A.

Graphic Design:
ART IQ, s. r. o.

Printed:
Česká typografie a. s.

Printed in the Czech Republic
Editor: Publishing house:

CORPORATION

Palachova Str. 957
252 63 Roztoky u Prahy
Tel./Fax: 20 91 13 81

ISBN 80-901958-1-4
EAN 978-80901958-1-3

MULDAU Fl